The Macmillan Book of

HOW THINGS WORK

ALADDIN BOOKS
Macmillan Publishing Company
866 Third Avenue, New York, NY 10022
Collier Macmillan Canada, Inc.

First Aladdin Books edition 1987

Printed in Hong Kong

A hardcover edition of *The Macmillan Book of How Things Work*
is available from Macmillan Publishing Company.

10   9   8   7   6   5   4   3   2   1

Photo on page 75 courtesy of *Renalife,* the journal of the National
Association of Patients on Hemodialysis and Transplantation.

The text of this book is set in 11 point Optima.
The illustrations are prepared in acrylic on acetate and reproduced in color and blackline.

Designed by Raúl Rodríguez

Library of Congress Cataloging-in-Publication Data

Folsom, Michael.
 The Macmillan book of how things work.

 Summary: Explains how many things such as plumbing,
telephones, automobiles, and x-ray machines work.
  1. Technology—Juvenile literature. [1. Technology]
I. Folsom, Marcia. II. Hamann, Brad, ill. III. Title.
IV. Title: How things work.
       T48.F56 1987   600   86-23761
       ISBN 0-689-71139-5

The Macmillan Book of

HOW THINGS WORK

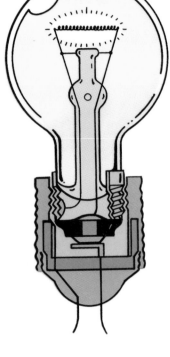

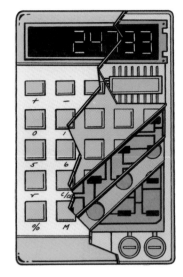

By Michael Folsom and Marcia Folsom

Illustrations by Brad Hamann

ALADDIN BOOKS
Macmillan Publishing Company
NEW YORK

Collier Macmillan Publishers
LONDON

Contents

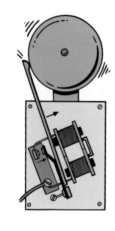

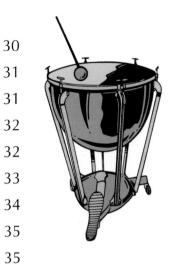

At Home

If you stopped to count how many electrical gadgets you use every day, you'd be amazed at the number.

Our lives would be completely different without electrical objects. They make life easier and more efficient.

Look around your home. What would it be like if there were fewer electrical objects—or no electricity at all?

Electrical System

Most of the machines and equipment that we use at home to make our lives easier and more enjoyable are powered by *electricity*. This power comes to our homes through a huge system of wires connected to a generator that creates the electricity. This system of wires connects each room of every house on every street, in every town and city, in every region of the country. The wires are carried on poles aboveground and in pipes below the ground.

These wires are always in pairs, because electric current has to flow in a complete path. One wire carries the electricity from the generator that produces the electricity. The other carries it back to the generator. Switches turn electrical devices off by breaking this complete flow of electricity. When switches are on, a meter measures the amount of electricity flowing to and from a building through the wires.

Generator A generator makes electricity by spinning a coil of metal wire close to a magnet. The magnetic force makes tiny atomic particles in the metal move as the coil spins past. These particles are called *electrons*. When the electrons move, electricity flows through the wire. Power comes from the force that spins the wire coil in the generator. The force can come from the weight of falling water that turns a wheel. It can also come from the power of expanding steam from boiling water. The water in an electric generating station can be boiled by burning coal or oil or gas. It can also be boiled by the heat of nuclear energy or by the energy of the sun or by heat from melted rock far below the surface of the earth.

Switch Everything that uses electricity has a switch to turn it on and off. When you turn a switch on, you close a "gate," completing a path in the electric circuit, so that electricity can flow through the wires.

Circuit Electric power in a house is divided into circuits. Each circuit is made up of separate pairs of wires going to separate parts of the house. If something goes wrong with electrical equipment in one part of the house, the electricity can still work in the other parts.

Fuse and Circuit Breaker Each circuit has a fuse or a circuit breaker. These are safety switches to prevent fires caused by too much electricity flowing through. If the wires or equipment on a circuit become too hot, these switches turn off the circuit automatically.

A fuse has a wire that heats up when electric current flows through it. When too much current flows through, the wire overheats and "blows" (melts), and the circuit is broken.

A circuit breaker is a spring-powered switch. If the metal trigger becomes too hot, it trips the switch, and the spring automatically shuts off the current to the circuit. There may be a red indicator that shows which circuit is broken.

After you fix the problem that made the circuit break, you can put in a new fuse or flip the circuit-breaker switch back on. Then the electricity will flow again through the circuit.

Meter All the electric current that comes into your house passes through a meter. The electricity drives a motor inside the meter. The motor turns faster when you use more electricity. The motor turns dials that record how much electricity you have used. The power company charges you for the amount shown on the meter.

switch

plug fuse

Side View

circuit breaker

(to reset push to *on* position)

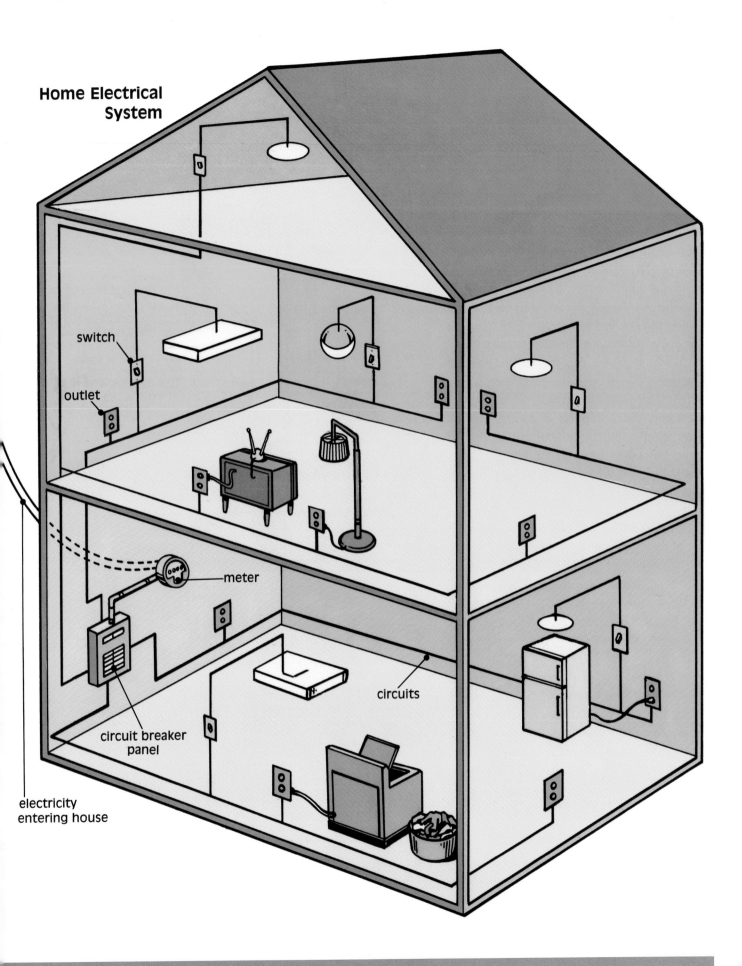

Home Electrical System

switch

outlet

meter

circuit breaker panel

circuits

electricity entering house

Lights

Light Bulb With a light bulb, electricity seems to turn night into day.

A metal called *tungsten* and a gas called *argon* make a light bulb work. The filament, a glowing wire inside the bulb, is made of tungsten. The bulb protects the glowing tungsten filament from burning up. In the air, the metal filament would combine with oxygen and burn. But the sealed bulb is filled with argon gas, which cannot combine with tungsten to burn. So the filament glows brightly for hundreds of hours.

Electricity makes the tungsten wire glow bright and hot. The wires that carry electricity usually allow the current to flow easily, like water through a big pipe. But if the wire is very thin, the electric power must force its way through. The thin wire resists the flow of the current.

This resistance is like friction, the action that makes your hands warm when you rub them together. When electricity meets resistance, its force can make a wire heat up. If the resistance is great enough, the wire becomes so hot that it begins to glow and shed light. This is called *incandescence.*

Light bulbs do "burn out," however. The filament doesn't really burn. It evaporates. Under the high heat of the electric current, even a tough metal can turn to vapor—like water turning to steam. The power of electricity makes tiny particles of the tungsten collide. Some of these particles are knocked free and float in the argon gas inside the bulb. Weak places develop in the filament, and finally the wire breaks. Burned-out bulbs often look discolored. The dark color is a thin film of evaporated tungsten that has coated the inner surface of the glass bulb.

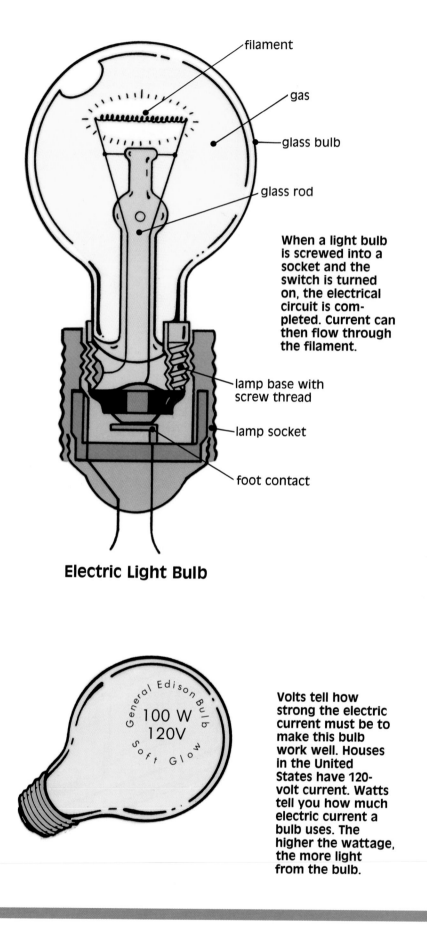

Electric Light Bulb

When a light bulb is screwed into a socket and the switch is turned on, the electrical circuit is completed. Current can then flow through the filament.

Volts tell how strong the electric current must be to make this bulb work well. Houses in the United States have 120-volt current. Watts tell you how much electric current a bulb uses. The higher the wattage, the more light from the bulb.

Fluorescent Light If you look closely at each end of the glass tube of a fluorescent light, you may see a little extra glow. These glowing spots are made by tiny tungsten filaments, like those in regular, or incandescent, light bulbs. When you turn on a fluorescent light, these wires light up.

The tungsten filaments warm up tiny particles of a metal called *mercury* that float inside the tube. When the mercury vapor is warm, electric current can flow through it from one end of the tube to the other. As the electricity flows through the mercury, the particles give off light.

Mercury-vapor light is invisible, but the inside of the tube is coated with a white chemical powder that glows when the invisible light hits it. This fluorescent glow is what we see.

Fluorescent Lamp

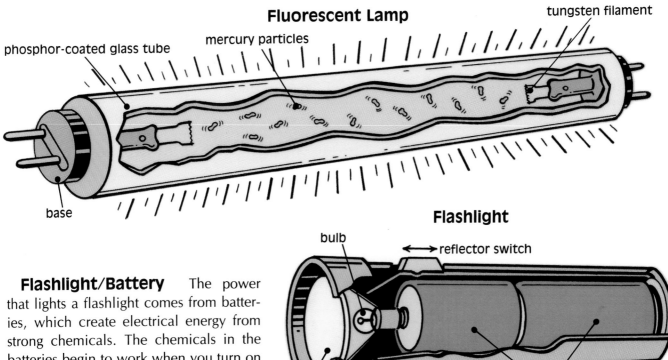

phosphor-coated glass tube

mercury particles

tungsten filament

base

Flashlight/Battery The power that lights a flashlight comes from batteries, which create electrical energy from strong chemicals. The chemicals in the batteries begin to work when you turn on the switch. The electricity then flows out of the battery, through the bulb, and back to the battery.

Most flashlight batteries have an outer container made of *zinc,* a metal, and an inner core of carbon. A chemical paste on the inside of the battery carries electric current. When the flashlight is on, the chemicals begin to eat away at the zinc on the outside of the battery, dissolving it. This action frees electrical particles in the zinc. They flow through the paste to the carbon, and then through the circuit to light the bulb. The zinc is slowly eaten up. In time the battery wears out.

Flashlight

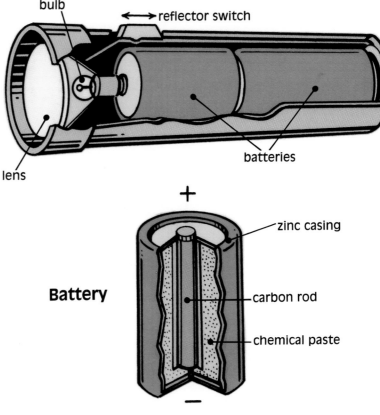

bulb

reflector switch

lens

batteries

Battery

+

zinc casing

carbon rod

chemical paste

−

Stove

Is the stove in your house gas or electric? Do you have a microwave oven? Each of these stoves uses a different form of energy to cook.

Electric Stove An electric stove gives off heat from current flowing through a thick wire called a *heating element*. The element gets hot in the same way the filament in a light bulb gets hot. But the heat is spread out through the thick wire, so it never gets hot enough to melt or burn the metal of the heating element.

The same kind of heating element that makes an electric stove work also works in many other home appliances. Toasters, electric coffee makers, hair dryers, electric water heaters, and electric blankets all have wire heating elements. Some houses are heated by electricity. They have radiators with heating elements in each room.

Rheostat As electricity flows to each heating element on a stove, it passes through a switch called a *rheostat*. In addition to turning electricity on and off, this switch can change the amount of electricity that goes through it. The more electricity, the higher the heat given off by the element. The rheostat lets you control the amount of heat that comes from each heating element and helps you cook your food at just the right temperature.

Rheostats are also used to dim electric lights and control the heat in electric blankets.

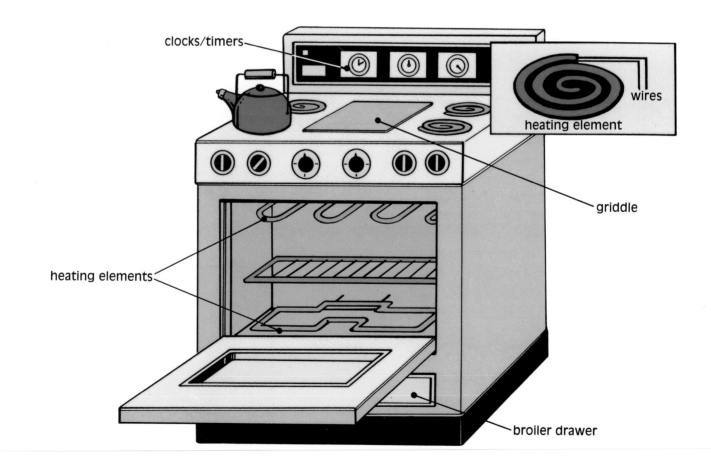

clocks/timers

wires

heating element

griddle

heating elements

broiler drawer

Gas Stove   Many homes use gas instead of electricity to get energy for cooking and heating. Gas comes into the house through a pipe from a storage tank. Sometimes this tank stands right outside the house. In cities, huge tanks, as tall as a 10-story building, store gas. From these tanks, gas goes through pipes under the streets to each house.

Pilot Light   Gas stoves often have a tiny flame that stays lit all the time. This flame lights the burner automatically when you turn the gas on. To conserve gas, some stoves have an electric starter that makes a small hot spark to light the burner.

Microwave Oven   How can a microwave oven bake a corn muffin in five minutes, when a regular oven takes five times as long?

In a regular gas or electric stove, waves of heat energy hit the outside of food. Then the heat gradually works its way inside. That is why roast beef can be well done on the outside and rare in the middle.

In a microwave oven, an electronic device turns a strong current of electricity into tiny (micro) waves of energy that radiate into the space inside the oven. These waves of energy zap right through food. A few waves hit the food and raise its temperature a little. But many of the waves slip through the food and pass out the other side. Microwaves cannot pass through metal, so they bounce off the metal insides of the oven and back through the food again. Each time this happens, the food gets hotter. The waves hit the inside parts of the piece of food just as often as the outside, so the heat is even. A piece of meat is cooked quickly and evenly—rare or well done all the way through.

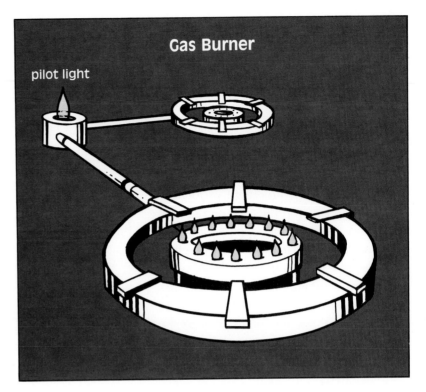

Gas Burner

pilot light

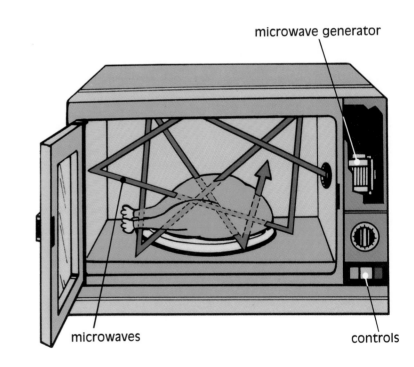

microwave generator

microwaves

controls

Refrigerator

A refrigerator makes food cold by taking the heat out of it. To do this, a refrigerator uses an electric motor, a kind of pump called a *compressor,* and a fluid called a *refrigerant.* The refrigerant changes from liquid to vapor when it boils, which happens easily because it has a very low boiling point. The compressor pumps the refrigerant through coiled pipes that run inside and, at the back, outside the refrigerator. As the fluid enters the coiled pipes inside the refrigerator, it boils and becomes vapor, able to take on heat. As the refrigerant reaches the pipes outside the refrigerator, it turns into liquid again and releases heat. Then the liquid travels back inside where it boils again and the vapor takes on more heat.

temperature control for refrigerator

temperature control for freezer

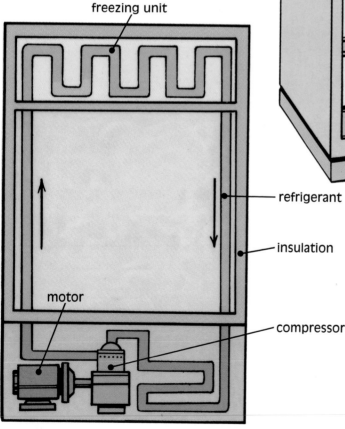

freezing unit

refrigerant

insulation

motor

compressor

Thermostat A thermostat is an automatic switch that turns heating and cooling devices on and off.

There are various kinds of thermostats. The most common kind is made of two kinds of metal joined together. These metals change their shape when they are heated or cooled. They expand when their temperature rises, and contract when it cools. Some metals expand and contract more than others. If you make a flat rod of two bonded metals, it will bend when the temperature changes. As the metal in a thermostat bends, it opens or closes an electric circuit. That's the way an ordinary switch moves when you push it with your finger.

Thermostat

warm

cool

electrical contacts

magnet

dial that sets temperature

bimetallic strip

Air Conditioner

Have you ever lived inside a refrigerator? If you have an air conditioner in your house, the answer is yes.

An air conditioner is a refrigerator that cools large spaces. The *cooling tube,* in which the refrigerant evaporates, juts into a room and takes on heat. The *radiating tube* is outside the house and gives off the heat from the room. One fan inside the air conditioner blows air into the room to cool it. A second fan blows air over the radiating tube to remove heat from the room. A thermostat regulates the air conditioner to keep the room as cool as you want it.

Air Conditioner

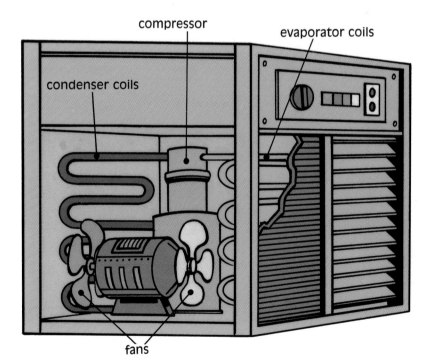

compressor

evaporator coils

condenser coils

fans

Doorbell

A doorbell uses electricity to make a hammer ring a bell. Electric current does this by creating a magnet that can turn on and off. If you wrap a piece of iron with a coil of wire and send electricity through the wire, the iron becomes a magnet—an *electromagnet*.

When you push the button to ring a doorbell, you turn on a switch that sends current to make an electromagnet work. The magnet attracts a hammer made of iron and makes the hammer strike the bell. But when the hammer moves, it opens another switch that breaks the current and turns off the electromagnet. A spring pulls the hammer back. When the hammer moves back, it closes the switch again, and the hammer strikes once more. *RING-NG-NG-NG-NG-NG-NG-NG!* As long as you keep your finger on the button, the electromagnet keeps turning itself on and off and the bell keeps ringing.

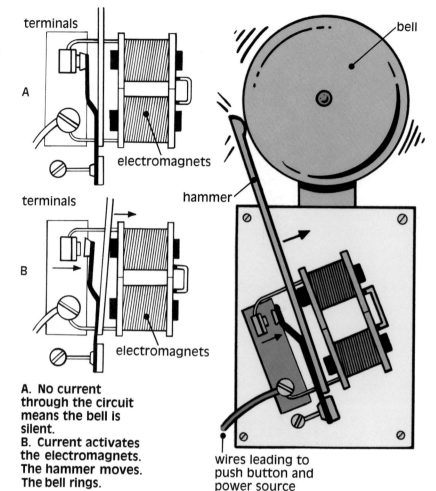

terminals

A

electromagnets

terminals

B

electromagnets

A. No current through the circuit means the bell is silent.
B. Current activates the electromagnets. The hammer moves. The bell rings.

bell

hammer

wires leading to push button and power source

Doorbell

Vacuum Cleaner

A vacuum cleaner has four main parts: an electric motor, a fan, a bag, and a tube. The motor turns the fan. The fan blows air out of the tube and creates a *partial vacuum* inside the tube. Air from outside rushes to fill that partially empty space. As the air rushes in, it picks up dirt. A bag made of cloth or paper inside the vacuum cleaner catches the dirt. The rushing air passes out through tiny holes in the cloth or paper. The dirt is collected in the bag.

Vacuum Cleaner

Electric Motor

An electric motor uses the power of magnetism to make a moving part, called a *rotor*, turn a shaft. This turning shaft can be attached to machines to make them work.

The rotor is an electromagnet that turns inside another magnet. These electromagnets, like all magnets, have a north pole and a south pole. (To get an idea of what poles are, think of a pencil. Make believe that the eraser end is the north pole and the point is the south pole.)

The opposite poles of the two magnets attract each other, and they come together. The north pole of one magnet attracts the south pole of the second. And the north pole of the second attracts the south pole of the first. When the magnets in a motor are attracted to each other, the rotor turns. The poles on the rotor's magnet keep switching back and forth. This keeps the rotor turning and makes the motor work.

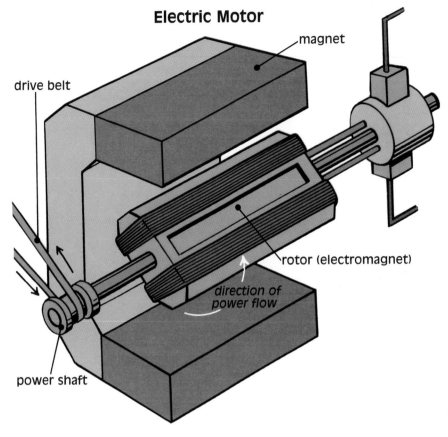

Electric Motor

magnet

drive belt

rotor (electromagnet)

direction of power flow

power shaft

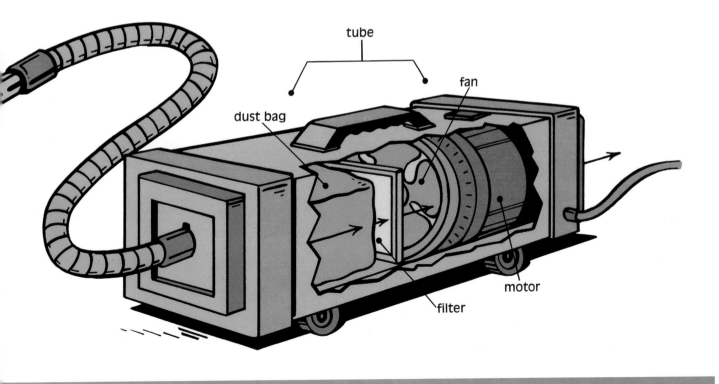

tube

fan

dust bag

motor

filter

Water System

The water we use flows in a system. This system is made up of four main parts:

1. A source of water
2. A way for the water to reach the house
3. A way for dirty water to drain away from the house and
4. A way to treat the dirty water so that it does not harm living things.

Some houses have their own water systems, with a well nearby and their own equipment for treating dirty water. But most houses now are part of a bigger system through which water is supplied to each home and waste water is treated in a sewage plant.

Reservoir Every water system starts with a way to collect and store as much water as we need. Usually this is in a reservoir, which is a lake created by a dam. Water flows downhill out of this lake when we need it. Sometimes it keeps flowing downhill through pipes that are connected directly to the faucets in houses. The weight of the water above the faucet is what forces water out.

Storage Tank If parts of a town or some of its buildings are higher than the level of the reservoir, water must be pumped uphill into a storage tank. You can often see these storage tanks atop hills or tall buildings. The water then flows from these tanks by the downward force of gravity.

Water Treatment Before water reaches your house, it is treated to make it safe to drink. Sand and dirt settle to the bottom of a tank. The water flows through a filter to take out smaller bits of dirt. Often chemicals are added to the water to kill germs that can make people sick. Many communities also add fluoride, a chemical that prevents tooth decay, to their water supply.

Sewer System Dirty waste water has to be carried away from the house. Large pipes underground take waste water away from areas where people live. These sewers connect to every house and run under the streets, out to a place where the sewage can be treated. Millions of gallons of waste water flow into a sewage treatment plant, which is made up of large tanks.

In some tanks, heavy particles settle to the bottom. From there the water goes to other tanks that contain bacteria. The bacteria turn the waste into material that is not dangerous to people. The bacteria need air to grow, so air is bubbled through the sewer water in this tank.

Some sewage plants add germ-killing chemicals to the waste water before it flows out into a river or ocean.

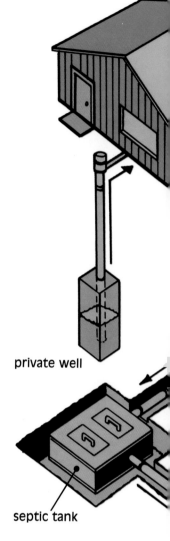

private well

septic tank

disposal field (sewage is spread out over a large area and is soaked into the ground)

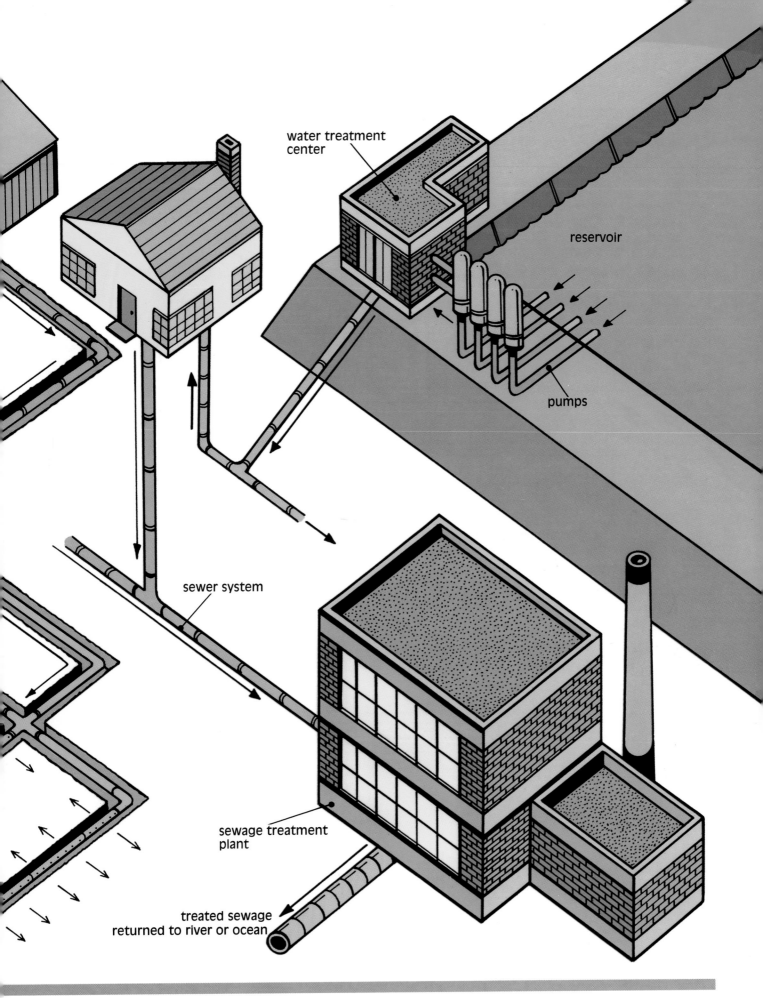

water treatment
center

reservoir

pumps

sewer system

treated sewage
returned to river or ocean

sewage treatment
plant

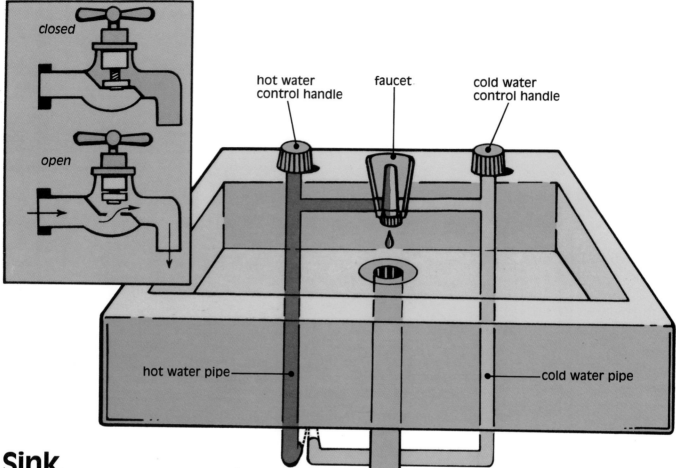

closed

open

hot water
control handle

faucet

cold water
control handle

hot water pipe

cold water pipe

drainpipe

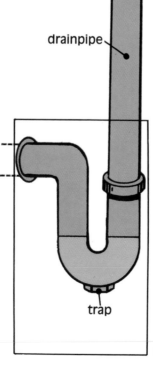

trap

Sink

A faucet is like a switch at the end of a pipe. A screw attached to a handle is inside most faucets. When you turn the handle, the screw twists up and lets the water in. When you turn off the water, the handle winds the screw back down. At the bottom of the screw is a flexible piece of rubber or plastic called a *washer*. It squeezes against the edges of the hole and keeps water from dripping.

The separate pipes for hot and cold water are often joined in one faucet with one spout. One such faucet works without screws. It has a ball with holes in it attached to a lever. When you push the lever to one side, the holes line up with hot or cold water pipes and give you the temperature you want. When you push the lever backward or forward, you change the amount of water that flows out of the faucet.

Have you ever wondered why the drainpipe below a sink always has a sharp U-bend in it? If you look closely, you can see that there is also a place to open the pipe at the bottom of the bend. This bend is called a *trap*. Water flows through it easily, but some water stays at the bottom. This water, trapped in the bend of the pipe, stops smelly gases in the sewer pipe from coming into the house. If the trap gets clogged, an adult can open the plug at the bottom and clean it out.

One other hidden part of the sink helps it work. The drainpipe going down to the sewer also has a vent pipe going up to the roof. This also helps keep sewer gases out of the house.

Washing Machines

Machines for washing clothes and dishes are kinds of sinks. They mix hot and cold water. They drain the dirty water out when the job is done. The water flow and the washing are done automatically.

The brain of an automatic washing machine is a clock that switches the water and the motor on and off. This clock also tells the machine how long it must work and when it should do different jobs such as washing and rinsing.

Clothes Washer A clothes washer cleans clothes by agitating them in soapy water. In a top-loading machine, wide blades beat up and down or back and forth inside a drum that holds the wash. In a front-loading machine, the drum revolves, tumbling the clothes over and over in the water to get them clean. Then the drum spins to force the water out and leave the wash nearly dry.

Dishwasher A dishwasher uses the power of spraying water. Water is first pumped into the washer and heated very hot. The pump then circulates the water through one or more rotating sets of arms full of spouts. Strong jets of water spray the dishes clean. The machine then pumps out the dirty water and pumps in new, clean water to rinse the dishes.

The water for washing machines comes from water pipes.

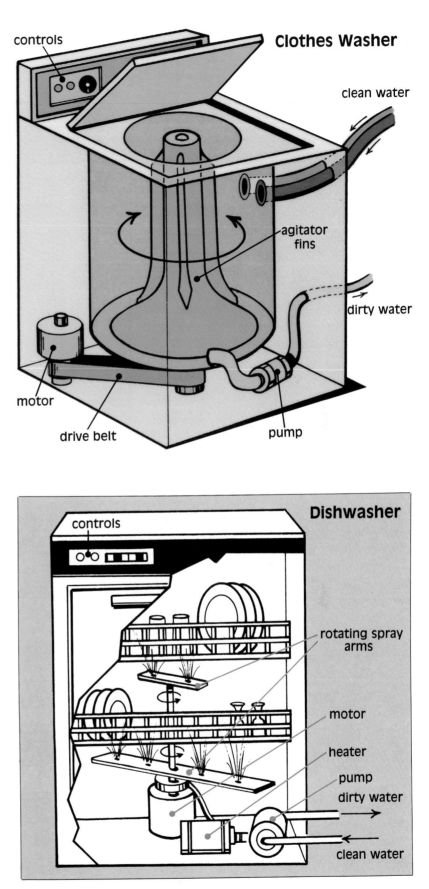

Clothes Washer

controls

clean water

agitator fins

dirty water

motor

drive belt

pump

Dishwasher

controls

rotating spray arms

motor

heater

pump

dirty water

clean water

Toilet

A toilet is a sink with a way of regulating how water flows in and drains out. You flush the toilet to set the machine in motion, but after that the mechanism works itself.

The bowl of a toilet is shaped to work like the trap under a sink. It stays full of water to keep sewer gas out of the house.

The force that works a toilet is the weight of falling water. The tank above the bowl collects about five gallons of water. That much water weighs about 40 pounds. When you turn or push the handle to flush the toilet, the water rushes into the bowl. This new water pushes the dirty water through the trap. New water fills the bowl again.

The tank stays open until all the water has drained out. Then a plug flops closed and a faucet lets new water flow in to refill the tank. This faucet is controlled by a floating handle. When the water in the tank rises, it pushes the handle up and gradually closes the inlet.

Many large buildings have toilets without separate tanks. Instead they have one large tank on the roof. The weight of all the water in this tank can push a high-powered rush of water into a toilet bowl when you flush it.

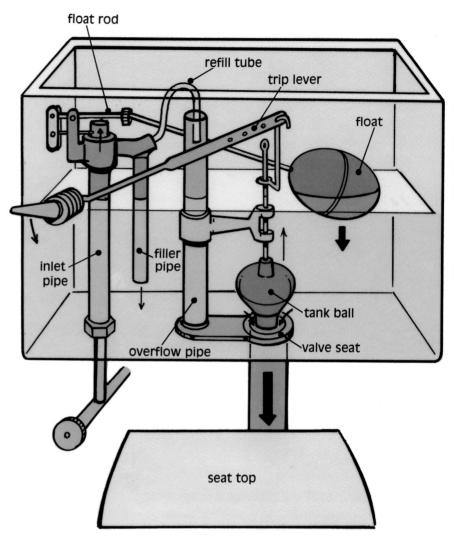

float rod
refill tube
trip lever
float
inlet pipe
filler pipe
overflow pipe
tank ball
valve seat
seat top

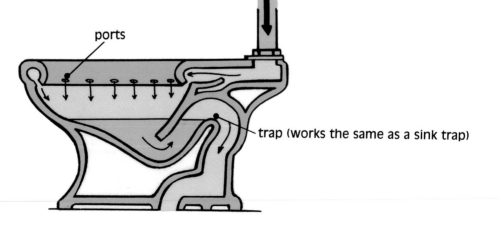

ports

trap (works the same as a sink trap)

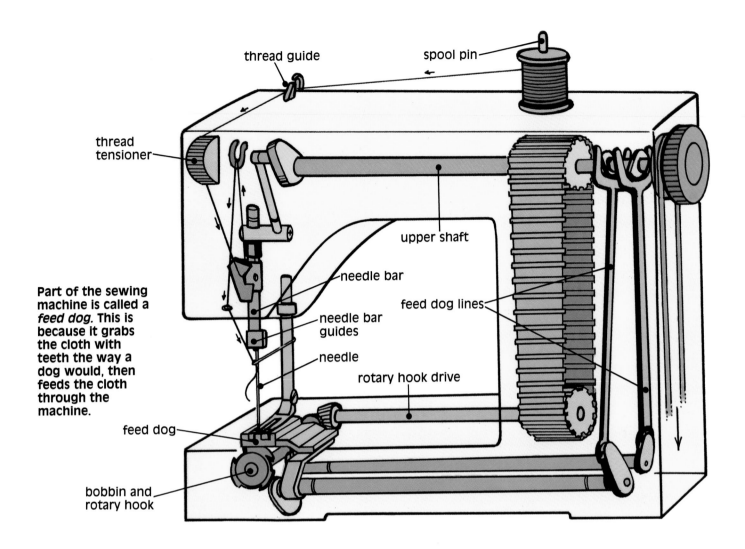

thread guide

spool pin

thread tensioner

upper shaft

needle bar

feed dog lines

Part of the sewing machine is called a *feed dog*. This is because it grabs the cloth with teeth the way a dog would, then feeds the cloth through the machine.

needle bar guides

needle

rotary hook drive

feed dog

bobbin and rotary hook

Sewing Machine

A sewing machine puts stitches into cloth by making tight little loops out of two threads coming from two separate spools.

One thread goes through an eye at the tip of the needle, which goes up and down through the cloth. Inside the machine, this thread makes a loop, and then a twirling hook makes the loop go around another thread that comes from below. When the needle jerks up again, the two threads are pulled tightly together, making a stitch. A jagged pusher moves the cloth ahead one short step at a time. Then the needle jerks down again to make another stitch . . . and another . . . and another . . .

How a Rotary Hook Works

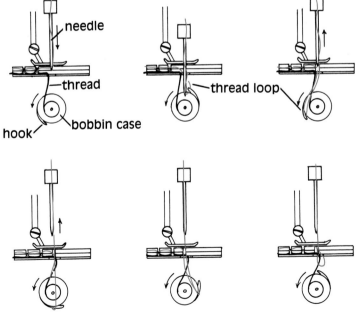

needle

thread

thread loop

hook

bobbin case

Clock

Clocks are complicated machines, yet they have only three basic parts to make them work: They have a source of power. They have a way to get that power from the source to the hands or the changing numbers that show the time. They have a way to regulate the speed at which the power is delivered, so that the time they show is always correct.

The power of mechanical clocks comes from the muscles of the person who winds up a spring or a weight. Most mechanical clocks are driven by a spring, though some large old-fashioned clocks still use the power of a falling weight. The weight is attached to a cable wound around a pulley.

The power of the windup clock turns gears that turn the hands to show the time. These gears transfer power from the source to the hands. They also change the speed of that power. The power comes from one source moving at one speed, but it must be delivered to the turning hands at three different speeds. The long minute hand must go around 12 times faster than the short hour hand, and the second hand must go around 60 times faster than the minute hand.

The speed in a mechanical clock is regulated by an *escapement*. This is a part that looks like a wide-open jaw trying to swallow a gear. At each end of the jaw is a sharp tooth. The jaw jerks back and forth around the gear, so that one tooth at a time bites into the gear. As that tooth jerks back out and escapes the gear on one side, the other tooth bites into the other side. Each time the teeth move in and out, the gear turns or advances by one notch.

The speed of the escapement jerking back and forth always has to stay the same.

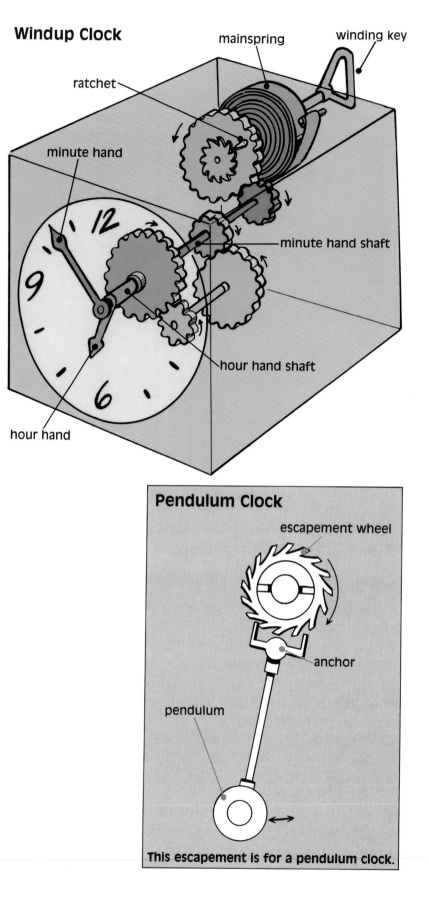

Windup Clock

winding key

mainspring

ratchet

minute hand

minute hand shaft

hour hand shaft

hour hand

Pendulum Clock

escapement wheel

anchor

pendulum

This escapement is for a pendulum clock.

That is how a clock keeps accurate time. One way to keep the movement the same is to attach the escapement to a swinging pendulum, with a weight hanging at the end of a rod. The power that drives the jaw of the escapement back and forth also moves the pendulum back and forth. The length of the pendulum regulates how fast the pendulum moves.

Another way to regulate the speed of an escapement is to attach it to a carefully balanced wheel connected to a tiny spring. The power of the clock swings the balance wheel around one way until the spring is wound up, then the power of the wound-up spring swings the wheel back the other way. Each swing takes the same amount of time as every other, and the clock tells the right time.

Electric Clock A clock driven by electricity has most of the same gears as a windup clock, but an electric clock has no escapement. The regulation of its speed is built into the electric power driving it.

The electricity that comes to our homes flows in two directions, back and forth through the wires. This is called alternating current. Each time the current switches its direction, the electromagnet rotor reverses its poles and keeps moving around. All electricity used in houses in the United States alternates 60 times each second. Electric clocks are made to use this speed.

Digital Watch A digital watch shows time in exact numbers. (Another word for number is *digit*.) Some digital watches are mechanical. They use a spring or electric motor to turn numbers that show the time. Most digital watches are powered by a tiny battery. Inside the watch is a tiny crystal of a stone called *quartz*. When electricity touches the quartz crystal, the crystal vibrates.

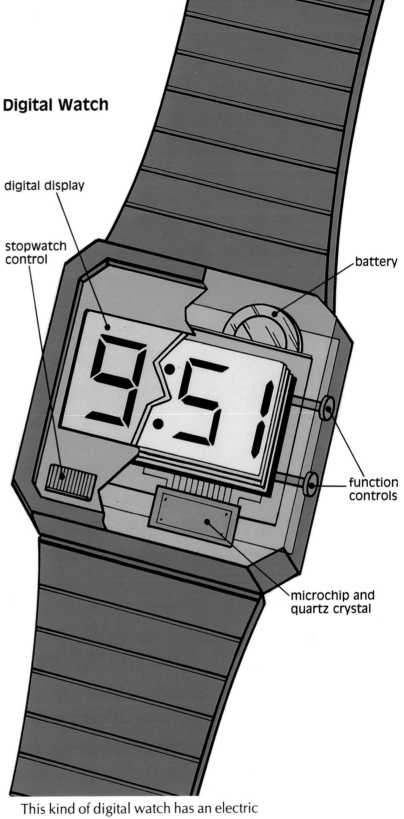

Digital Watch

digital display

stopwatch control

battery

function controls

microchip and quartz crystal

This kind of digital watch has an electric counter that counts vibrations per second. Whenever the counter gets to a certain figure, it sends a signal to the display on the face of the watch. At each signal, one second is added to the number on the face of the watch.

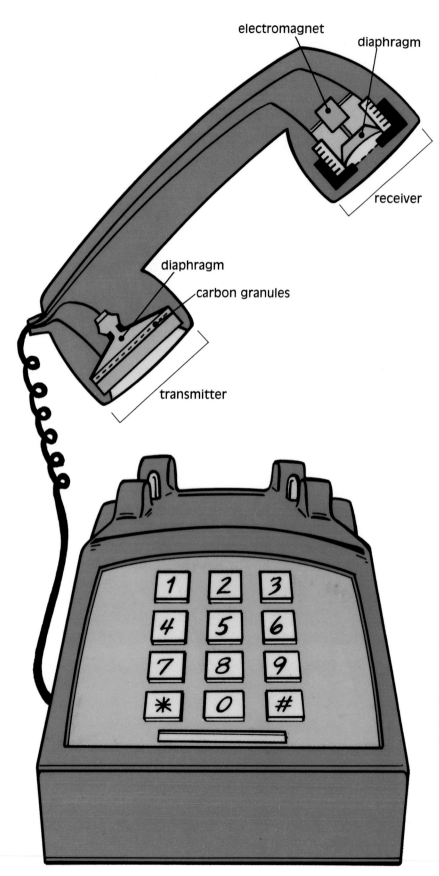

electromagnet

diaphragm

receiver

diaphragm

carbon granules

transmitter

Telephone

A telephone is a translating machine. It translates our words from a language of air into a language of electricity.

When you speak, your voice box, or *larynx*, vibrates. This creates sound waves that move through the air. Inside a person's ear is a thin skin called a *diaphragm*. The diaphragm vibrates when sound hits it. This vibration in a listener's ear communicates the sound of your voice, and the listener's brain translates it into meaningful words.

But spoken sounds do not travel very far in the air. The vibrations spread out in every direction and quickly weaken. The telephone makes it possible to direct your voice exactly where you want it to go, just about anywhere in the world. Electricity makes this possible. When you talk on the phone, the vibrations of your voice are turned into pulses of electricity. At the other end of the phone, the pulses of electricity are turned back into air vibrations.

The handset of the telephone holds the parts that do the translating. The mouthpiece has a microphone. The microphone is filled with grains of carbon that look like fine black sand. A current of electricity passes through the microphone following a path made by carbon grains that touch together. When you speak into the microphone, your voice vibrations squeeze the carbon grains into various patterns. In that way they keep changing the strength of the electric current. The pattern of weak and strong waves of current is the same as the pattern of your voice vibrations.

The part of the phone that you hold against your ear contains a metal disc. It is attached to an electromagnet. The electrical voice waves turn the magnet on and off. This makes the metal disc vibrate. The vibrations move the air and a voice can be heard.

Two different devices, using a dial or buttons, make sure your voice gets to the right telephone.

One device is the old-fashioned rotary dial. You turn the dial with your finger. When you let go, a spring turns back the dial. This action sends a number of electrical signals out over telephone wires. The telephone number you reach depends on how far you have turned the dial.

These electrical signals flip switches in the telephone company office. Each switch connects with other switches. If you dial 555-0987, the first signals will get you to the switch for all phones with numbers starting with 5. Your second twist of the dial will get you through the 5 switch to the switch for all phones with numbers that start in 55. This goes on until you have reached the one phone in 10 million that has the exact seven numbers in the order you want. *Ring! Ring!*

Newer telephones, which have buttons to push instead of a dial to turn, work faster. On a dial phone, the number *9* takes longer to dial than the number *1*, but on a push-button phone, all numbers take the same time. These phones use a combination of musical sounds rather than a series of electrical signals, to tell the equipment which switches to connect.

Radio

Radio starts at a microphone that changes voice vibrations into electrical signals. Radio ends with a speaker that turns electrical waves back into vibrations in the air that carry the sounds to your ear.

The electrical signals from the microphone go to a *transmitter* that sends the electrical signals out through the air over long distances without any wires. The transmitter uses a very strong electric current. The transmitter gives this current a steady signal of its own. This signal is in the form of pulses or waves getting stronger and weaker a certain number of times every second.

Each radio station has its own wavelength, which is called its frequency, or wave band. *Frequency* means how many times the wave goes from strong to weak and back again each second. Assigning these different radio frequencies to all the stations keeps their messages separate, so that they don't get mixed up.

The radio transmitter broadcasts this frequency from an antenna. The antenna is usually a tall metal tower. At the top of the antenna, the electrical energy actually jumps from the wires and radiates out through the air. The waves move out in every direction from the antenna—like ripples in a pond radiating from the place where a pebble drops. Close to the top of the tower this radiation is strong, but the energy of the radio waves gets weaker and weaker as it moves farther away. Because there are many radio stations around the world, the air is full of electrical radio waves. These waves are weak, and we cannot detect them.

Before the radio waves are transmitted, however, something else has to happen. The transmitter takes the weak electrical signals that come from the microphone and mixes them with the strong steady signal of the radio frequency. In that way, the steady signal carries the changing signal that comes from the microphone.

At the other end of the radio system is the *receiver*. When we say we have a radio at home, we mean we have a radio receiver. It has an antenna, too. Sometimes the antenna sticks out of the radio's housing, but often it is a loop of wire inside the box. The antenna picks up the radio frequencies from all the stations close enough to hear, and feeds them into the receiver.

When you move the dial, you are working the *tuner* inside the receiver. When you choose a station with the dial, the weak radio signal goes to an *amplifier*. A strong electrical current flowing through the amplifier picks up the patterns of the radio waves. It makes them stronger and sends them to a *speaker*.

The speaker in a radio, like the earpiece of a telephone, translates electrical waves back into vibrations in the air. To control the loudness of the sounds coming from the speaker, you turn a knob. It controls the strength of the electrical signal going to the speaker.

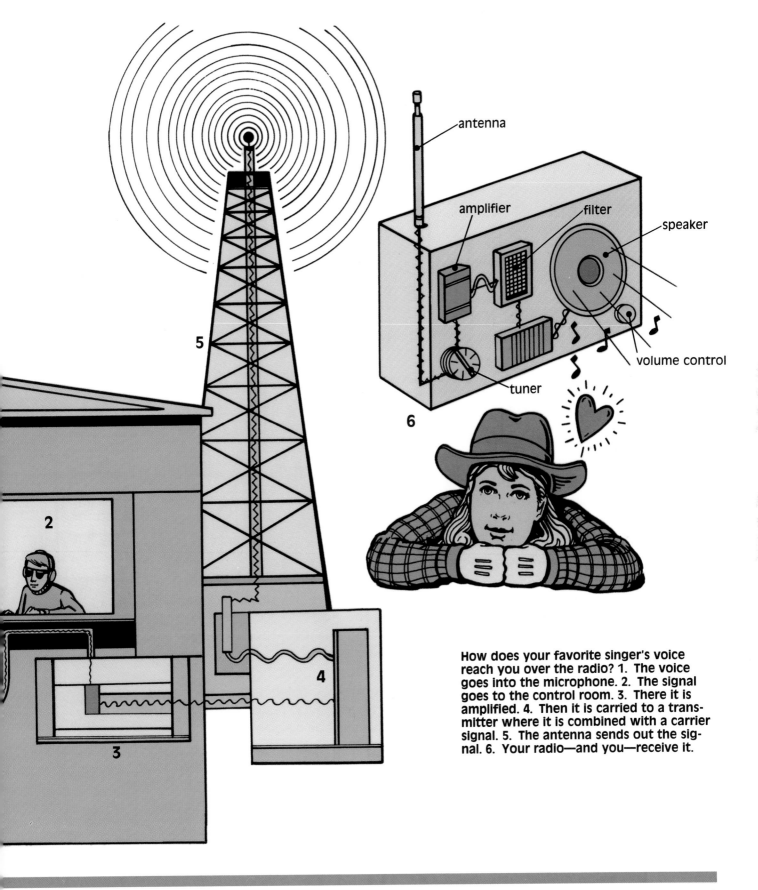

antenna

amplifier   filter   speaker

5

tuner   volume control

6

2

3   4

How does your favorite singer's voice reach you over the radio? 1. The voice goes into the microphone. 2. The signal goes to the control room. 3. There it is amplified. 4. Then it is carried to a transmitter where it is combined with a carrier signal. 5. The antenna sends out the signal. 6. Your radio—and you—receive it.

Camera

The photographic camera uses light and chemicals to make a record of a scene. A camera is a tight box with two important parts. One part is an opening that lets in just the right amount of light. The second part is a film with chemicals that change when light hits them.

The part of a camera that lets in light combines a *shutter* and a *lens*. The shutter opens a hole in the camera, and then shuts it again. A shutter can open and close again very quickly. The size of the hole and the time it stays open determine how much light gets in.

The lens shapes the way the light travels through the hole, so that you get a picture, not just a blur of light. The lens is a carefully curved magnifying glass or set of glasses. The lens focuses the light that comes from the scene you see outside the camera, and makes the same scene appear inside the camera.

The lens focuses the picture directly on the film inside the camera. The patterns of light in the picture make the chemicals in the film change. The chemicals have been spread through the transparent film that you load into the camera. With black-and-white film, the parts of the film that are hit by light turn dark. The other parts stay clear. With color film, different layers of the film change according to the amount of each color of light that hits them. For example, one layer will change when blue light hits it, but not when red light comes through. The changes in all the layers blend and give you a picture that looks true to life.

The film usually has to be taken out of the camera in a dark place. Then the film must be washed in chemical baths so that the changes in the film become permanent. This is called *developing* the film.

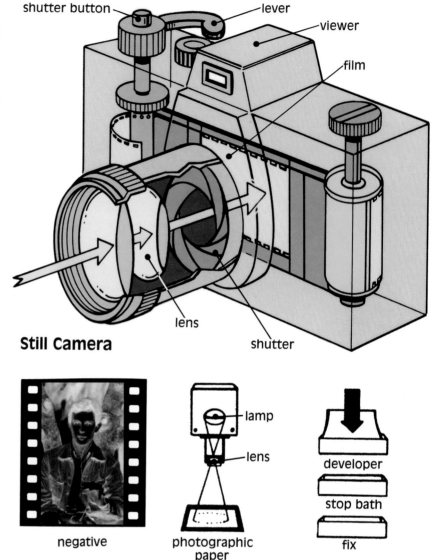

Still Camera

negative

lamp
lens
photographic paper

developer
stop bath
fix

The result is a *negative*. A negative is a transparent film on which your picture appears with the light and dark areas reversed. A bright light is a black spot. A dark shadow is clear.

To make a positive print, the transparent negative film is projected through another lens onto photographic print paper that also has chemicals on it. These chemicals change according to the patterns of light and dark in the negative. Areas that were dark in the negative come out light on the positive print. The print paper is then developed in baths of chemicals. The result is a permanent picture.

photo

Instant Photography Some cameras take pictures and develop the film, too. In these instant cameras, the lens and shutter work the same way as those in a regular camera, but the film is more complicated. Instant black-and-white film has both the transparent negative and the print paper packed closely. After you take a picture, you wind the film forward, and a packet of chemicals is squeezed open. These chemicals ooze over the negative film and the print paper. When you open the package you peel off the finished print. With instant color film, all the chemical changes go on inside a thin sealed package of film. The package has one transparent side. As the chemicals develop, the color picture becomes visible on the outside.

Movie Camera A movie camera is much like a still camera that takes moving pictures. The only real difference is that a moving picture camera takes a great many small photographs on a long roll of film in a short time. Most movie cameras take 18 or 24 pictures every second. An electric motor winds the film past the lens and shutter with a jerky motion. The film actually stops moving when the shutter opens to take a picture. Then the winder quickly jerks another frame of film in front of the shutter, ready to take another picture.

Movie film is always printed on other transparent film, not on solid print paper. That way, light going through the transparent film can project the pictures onto a screen. In a movie projector, a motor moves the film at the same speed it moved in the camera, and with the same kind of jerky motion. A shutter opens and closes so that only the still picture is projected. You don't see the film moving. But because so many still pictures are shown one after another so quickly, they all seem to blend. A viewer gets the sense that scenes in the pictures are moving.

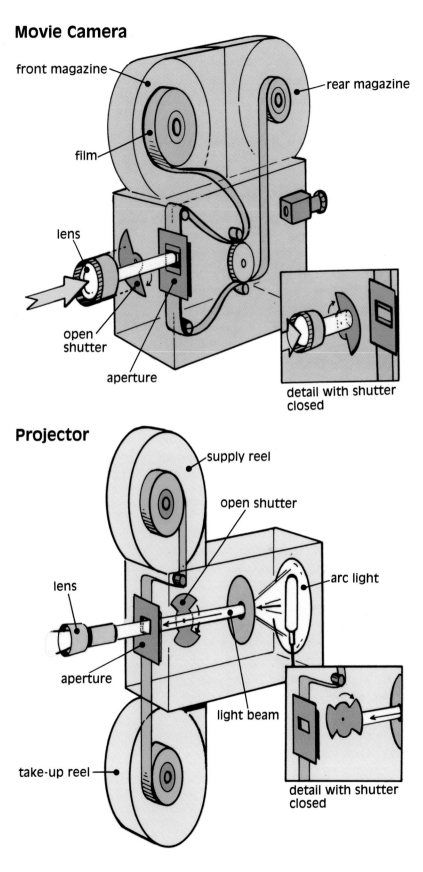

Movie Camera

front magazine

rear magazine

film

lens

open shutter

aperture

detail with shutter closed

Projector

supply reel

open shutter

arc light

lens

aperture

light beam

take-up reel

detail with shutter closed

Television

Television translates both light waves and sound vibrations into electrical messages. This combination sends a talking picture through space.

A television camera, like a photographic camera, has a lens that focuses a picture on a surface inside the camera. But the two kinds of cameras are different. In a television camera, the surface that picks up a picture is inside the end of a glass tube. This surface is coated with chemicals that change when light hits them. Inside the tube is a "gun" that "shoots" a beam of electric particles at the back of this chemically coated surface. The beam picks up the pattern of light and dark that the lens makes on the chemicals. The beam of electrical particles then bounces back to the gun. From there, the electrical signals are transmitted in radio waves from an antenna.

Color TV Camera The tube in a television camera can pick up only the difference between light and dark in a picture. It cannot tell the difference between colors. Then how can we have color television?

A color television camera is really three cameras in one. The lens focuses the picture on three separate tubes. Each tube has a color filter that lets in only one color of light—red, blue, or green. The television transmitter broadcasts electrical messages for three separate black-and-white pictures. Each one is different, because the amounts of red, blue, and green light in the original picture were different. When these electric messages are received by a color television set, the receiver mixes the information together and creates a color picture on the screen.

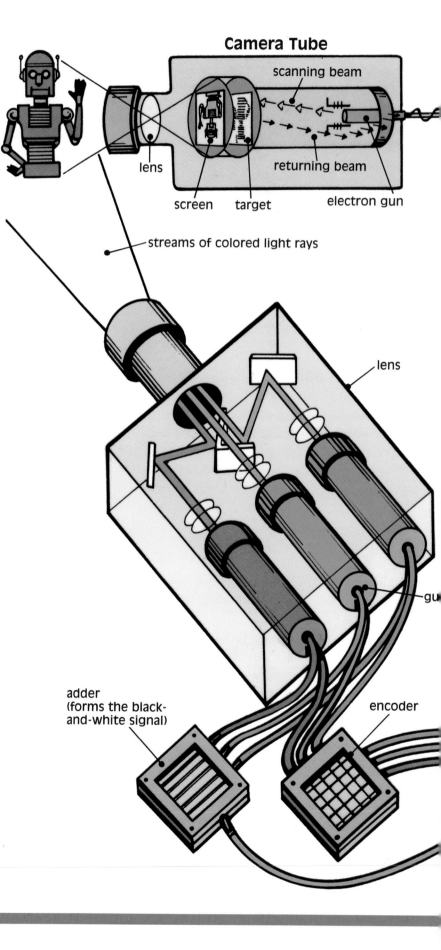

Camera Tube

scanning beam

lens

screen   target

returning beam

electron gun

streams of colored light rays

lens

gu

adder
(forms the black-
and-white signal)

encoder

TV Set A television, like a radio, picks up sound signals from a video program. The video receiver also picks up the picture messages and changes them back into the original form, a picture we can see. But it is much more complicated to translate electric messages into a picture than into sound.

The *video,* or picture, system can't handle an entire picture at once. The camera has to break the picture down into tiny pieces. The receiver puts them together.

In the camera, the gun sweeps its beam of electric particles back and forth across the light-sensitive screen one line at a time from top to bottom. The electric beam goes back and forth many times to take in one entire picture. It does this 30 times each second. In this way, television and movies are similar. They both use many individual pictures coming very fast, one after the other, to create a moving picture.

The most important part of the TV set, or receiver, is the picture tube where ev-erything is put back together again. There is a gun inside this tube, too. It shoots out electric particles that sweep across the screen in exactly the same pattern used by the gun in the camera. On the inside of the screen there is a layer of light-sensitive chemicals, like the chemicals inside a fluorescent light tube, but more complicated. When the electrons hit the chemicals, the chemicals glow and give off light—a lot or a little, depending on the pattern of the original picture.

A color TV picture tube contains three guns. Each shoots a beam of electric particles for one of the three colors. The screen is coated with tiny clusters of three dots of three different chemicals. One glows red, one blue, and one green. Each gun is aimed at the dots for its color. The dots light up with more or less brightness, depending on the color and patterns of brightness in the original picture. Your eye puts these dots together as a continuous colored picture.

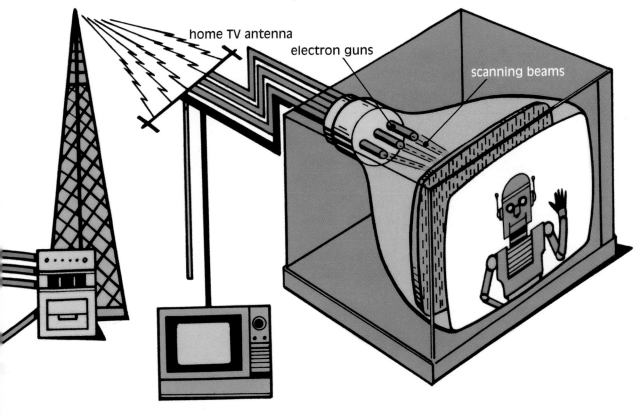

home TV antenna

electron guns

scanning beams

Phonograph

Phonograph means *sound writing*. The phonograph was the first invention that could make a permanent record of sounds and play them back again.

The phonographic recorder changes the vibrations of sound in the air into the vibrations of a sharp needle, or *stylus,* that cuts a groove in the plastic surface of a disc. A microphone picks up the vibrations in the air and turns them into waves of electrical current. These waves control an electromagnet that moves the cutting needle very quickly from side to side as the disc spins. With the needle, the sound vibrations cut a wiggly groove that spirals from the outside to the inside of the record.

The record player turns the wiggles in the record's grooves back into sound. The player's needle rides lightly in the groove of a record. The wiggles make the needle vibrate and produce signals that are carried by electricity through the phonograph's speakers.

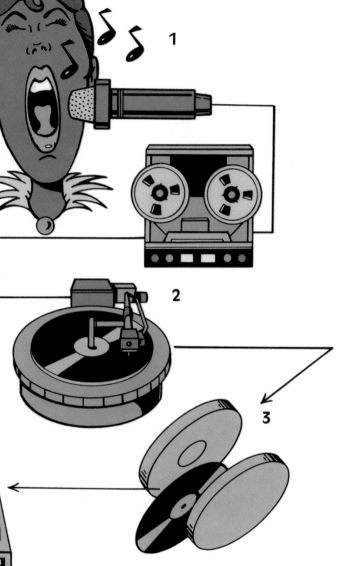

cartridge
stylus(needle)
record grooves

1. The microphone changes sound into electrical signals.

2. A master disc is made by a needle that cuts a groove.

3. Stampers, which are metal-coated molds of the master disc, are used to press the two sides of a plastic phonograph record.

Tape Recorder

A tape recorder stores words and music in a magnetic language. The plastic tape in a tape recorder has a layer of tiny particles of an iron compound that is similar to rust. The job of the recording machine is to magnetize those particles, some more than others, in a pattern that matches the pattern of air vibrations of the sound you want to record.

The tape in a tape recorder works like the spiral grooves of a phonograph record. It is wound on a wheel. As it records or plays, it winds off that wheel and onto another. Most home tape recorders now use a cassette to hold these two wheels with their tape. This small plastic case keeps everything inside, so that the tape cannot come loose.

A tape recorder takes the electrical signals from a microphone and turns them into magnetic signals. The tape winds past a small metal part called the *recording head* and rubs against it. Inside the recording head, there is a tiny electromagnet. It becomes stronger or weaker depending on the amount of electricity coming from the microphone, which changes voice vibrations into electrical signals. The variations in the strength of the magnetism in the head are transferred to the tape as the tape moves past.

When you want to play back the recording on the tape, the tape moves past the playing head. The magnetic signals on the tape create a tiny electrical current in a coil of wire inside the playing head. The variations in the electrical current made by the magnetic pulses go to an amplifier and then to a speaker so they can be heard.

Videocassette Recorder
A VCR is a tape recorder that can turn into magnetic signals all the information that makes

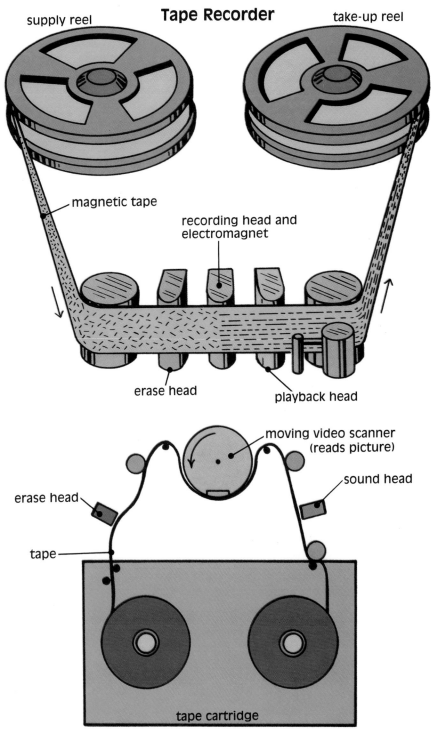

Tape Recorder

supply reel • take-up reel • magnetic tape • recording head and electromagnet • erase head • playback head

moving video scanner (reads picture) • sound head • erase head • tape • tape cartridge

Videocassette Recorder

sound and pictures on a TV set. Because this requires a lot more information than just the sound alone, the tape in a videocassette is much wider than the tape in a sound-recording cassette.

Laser Disc

Laser disc recorders and players use a beam of *laser light* to change a computer code into sounds and pictures.

A laser disc looks something like a phonograph record without grooves. Beneath the shiny, smooth surface of the disc is a round metal sheet. This sheet has a spiral track made of tiny round depressions called *pits*. In the factory, these pits are eaten out of the metal by chemicals.

When you play a laser disc, a beam of laser light follows this track of pits. A beam of laser light is sharp and accurate. It doesn't spread out like light from a bulb. When light hits the shiny flat part of the metal disc, it reflects back to a light-sensitive detector. When the laser beam shines on a pit, it doesn't reflect back. The detector turns the on-and-off flashes of reflective light into electrical signals.

A computer in the laser disc player reads the pattern of on-and-off electrical signals. The computer has a memory that stores every possible combination of the ons and offs on the track. The computer can turn this code back into sounds and pictures.

A laser disc that plays only sound is called a *compact disc* (CD). It is less than five inches across and can play more music than a long-playing phonograph record. The disc spins as many as 500 times a minute while the beam of laser light reads. The spiral track of pits on a CD is less than 1/100,000th of an inch wide. More than 100,000 tracks fit in an inch. The pits on the surface of this track store 600 million separate pieces of computer information. One compact disc can store all the words in an entire encyclopedia.

Video discs are larger than CDs—usually 12 inches across. They can store 54,000 individual pictures, enough to record a full-length movie.

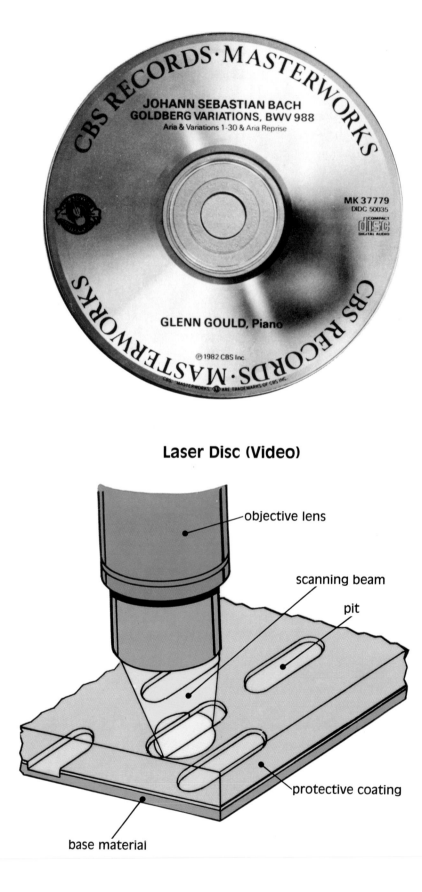

Laser Disc (Video)

- objective lens
- scanning beam
- pit
- protective coating
- base material

Video Disc

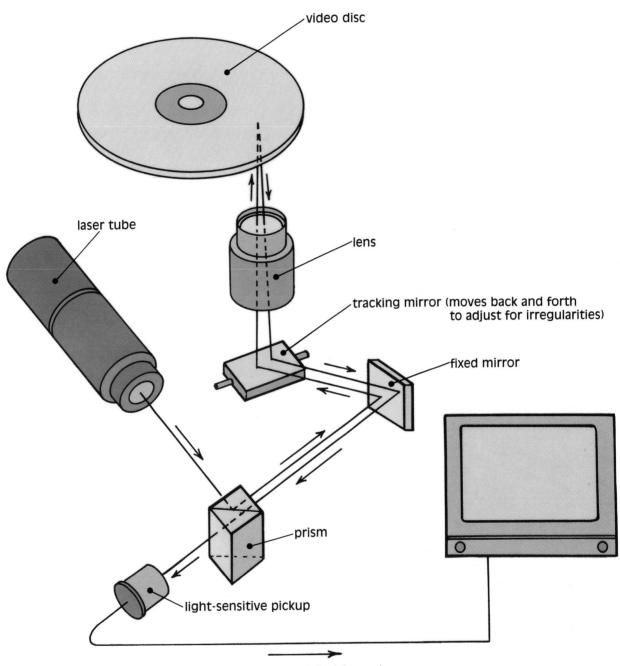

video disc

laser tube

lens

tracking mirror (moves back and forth
to adjust for irregularities)

fixed mirror

prism

light-sensitive pickup

signal travels to television set

At Work

Running a toy store must be a lot of fun. It's also rather easy, thanks to the help of machines.

Computers keep track of money coming in and bills to be paid, of merchandise on shelves and what must be ordered.

Typewriter

The typewriter was the first important office machine. A speedy typist can write 60 to 100 words per minute, and even more. A fast writer can write only about 30 words a minute by hand.

When you write with a typewriter, five basic movements are involved. First you press a *key* with your finger. This moves levers to make a type bar jump up and strike an inked ribbon against the paper. The ink prints a letter on the paper that is wrapped around the roller on the carriage. You can also *shift* the type bars up and down. Each type bar has two letters on it, a capital letter and small letter. You use the shift level to choose which one you want. When you strike a key or hit the space bar, you advance the paper sideways one space. The paper moves with the carriage, which is pulled by a spring along a set of rails. To start a new line, you return the carriage to the right side of the typewriter. This turns the roller up at the same time to start a new line.

Electric Typewriter   The first big improvement in the mechanical typewriter was electrification. Some electric typewriters have no moving carriage. The paper still goes around a roller. But the type is all contained on the surface of a light hollow ball. This ball moves along the paper from one side to the other. There is no mechanical connection between the key you hit and the type piece that hits the ribbon. Each key sends its own electrical message to the type ball mechanism. This message makes the ball turn so that the character you want typed is facing the paper. Then the type ball jumps forward to strike the ribbon and paper.

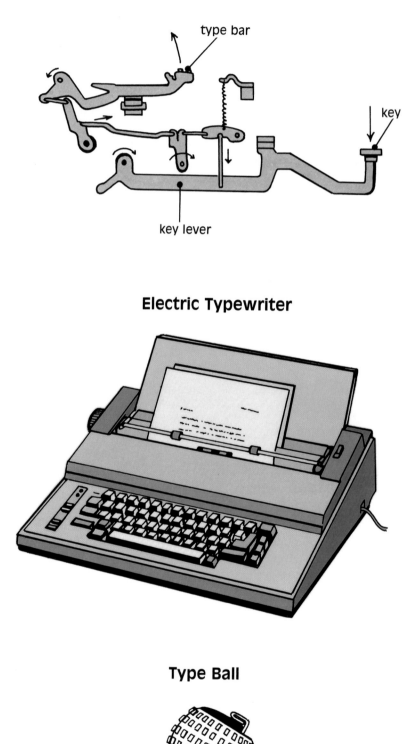

type bar

key

key lever

Electric Typewriter

Type Ball

Calculator

An electronic calculator is a small computer that solves arithmetic problems. It works at the speed of light, and can give you an answer faster than you can explain the problem.

A tiny piece of the mineral called *silicon* makes a calculator work. Silicon has certain properties that allow it to vary the way it conducts electricity.

In a calculator, three super-thin layers of silicon are put together. The middle layer changes, depending on how strong a current of electricity flows to it. If it gets a strong current, it becomes a good conductor, and another current can flow easily from one outside layer to the other. If the middle layer gets a weak current, it stops the current between the outside layers. In other words, silicon acts as an electric switch.

The electronic calculator's brain is a chip of layered silicon smaller than a postage stamp and as thin as a dime. Even in this small area, the chip has hundreds of thousands of switches arranged in rows. Each of these switches can go on and off a half million times a second.

The switches in an electronic chip can count only two numbers—0 and 1. But with those two numbers, you can make a code for 0 through 9 with a few switches. With these numbers, all the rest can be made. Each number has a code. The code *11*, for example, stands for the number *3*.

If you push the + key, that creates a pattern of switches that tells the calculator to add the next number to the earlier ones already memorized in the pattern of on-off switches. When you push the = key, the "equals" code directs the calculator to look for all the stored numbers controlled by the "plus" code. In almost no time, the answer flashes on the display.

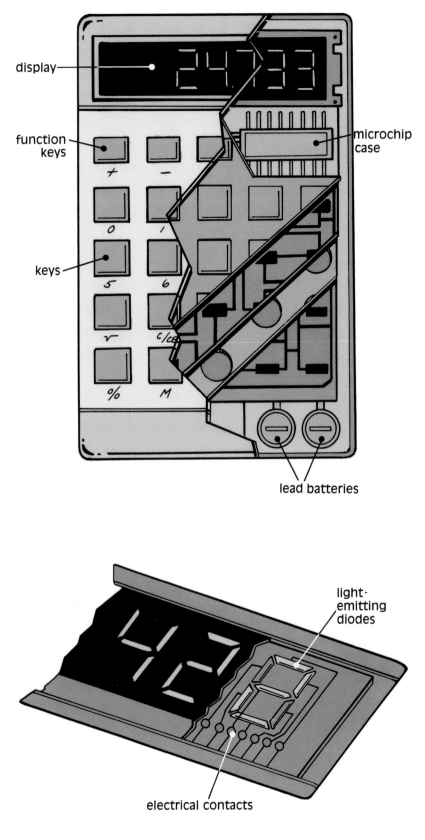

display — function keys — keys — microchip case — lead batteries — light-emitting diodes — electrical contacts

Word Processor

A word processor looks like a cross between a typewriter and a television set. It has a keyboard. Its printer moves paper around a roller and types letters on the paper with ink. It also has a video screen, where the words you enter appear before they are printed.

A word processor is basically a computer that uses the same kind of lightning-fast language of a number code found in an electronic calculator. Each of the letters of the alphabet is assigned a pattern of on-and-off switches in the silicon chips that make the word processor work.

A word processor has a memory. Each letter in on-and-off code goes into the electronic memory of the processor. If you want to change a letter or word that you have entered, you can. You just push a button to make the change in the machine's memory.

In order to store a large amount of writing, words in on-and-off code are recorded on a magnetic disc. This disc is like a cross between a phonograph record and a tape recorder. Information is stored on it magnetically in a spiral pattern, like music in the grooves on a phonograph record. The

disc has one great advantage over tape. The computer can move back and forth across the surface of the disc and go instantly to any place from the beginning to the end. This way it can find information quickly.

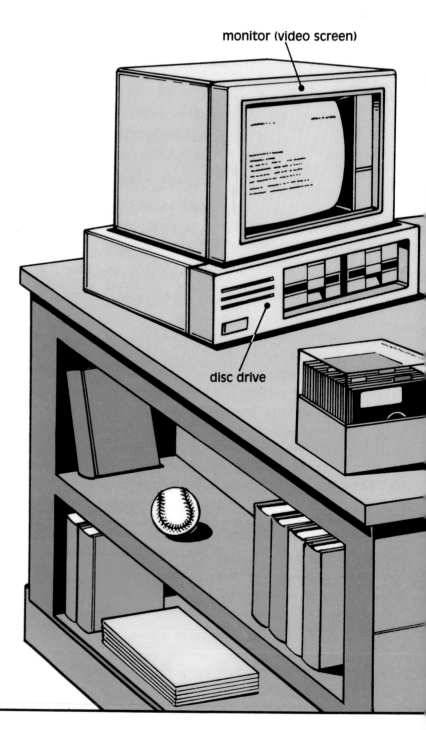

monitor (video screen)

disc drive

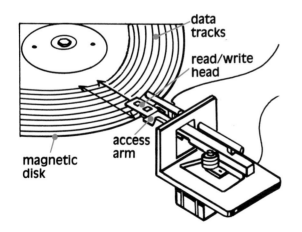

data tracks

read/write head

magnetic disk

access arm

printer

keyboard

floppy disc

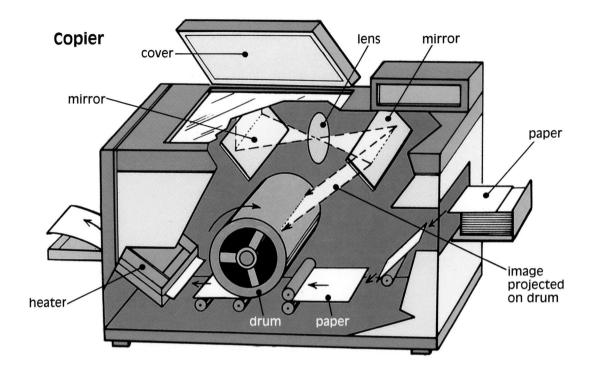

Copier

cover

mirror

lens

mirror

paper

heater

drum

paper

image projected on drum

Copying Machine

Most photocopiers are a kind of printing machine that uses dry ink in a process called *xerography*. (*Xero* in ancient Greek means *dry*.) Xerography makes it possible to print almost anything on plain paper instantly.

When you put a piece of paper on the glass plate on top of a copying machine, you are getting ready to take a picture. A very bright light sweeps across the underside of the plate. In that light, a picture of what is on the paper can be focused through a lens onto a light-sensitive surface inside the machine—just as a camera focuses a picture on the surface of the film. Unlike a camera, however, a copier doesn't take a whole picture at once. Only a thin slice of the picture is focused at any one time. And the surface on which it is focused moves while the picture is being taken. This surface is actually the outside of a metal drum which is as smooth and silvery as a mirror. This drum turns as the

light sweeps across the paper being copied. In that way, the entire picture is focused on the surface of the drum with each full turn. Every time the drum turns, another picture is taken and another copy is made.

The important thing is to have the picture stick instantly to the surface of the drum, and then be wiped off quickly. Electricity and a colored powder make these quick changes possible. The surface of the drum is charged with electricity. Wherever light hits the surface, the electric charge becomes lower. Whatever is dark on your original page stays charged with electricity on the turning drum of the copier. Colored powder is dusted on the surface of the drum. The powder sticks wherever the electric charge remains strong. A piece of blank paper rolls through and the powder is transferred to the surface of the paper. The paper is heated to melt the powder and make it stick. The sheet with its pattern of melted powder is your copy. The entire surface of the drum is once again charged with electricity, and it is ready for the next page to copy.

Cash Register

A modern cash register is an electronic calculator with a drawer to keep money in. When your bill is added up, the money drawer slides open so that the clerk can make change and put money safely away.

Universal Product Code Almost everything for sale in the United States now comes in a package marked according to the Universal Product Code (UPC) system. Every item has its own coded message in a series of bars or lines. There are 30 bars altogether, some thick and some thin. Some are farther apart than others. The coded messages of these bars tell the exact name and size of the product and the name of the company that made it. The code is also shown in numbers, so that store workers can identify it without a computer.

An automatic reader for the price code is built into the check-out counter at the grocery store. The check-out clerk slides the package marked with the code over a set of slots in the counter. Light flashes through these slots and reflects back through the slots to the reader, which changes the code pattern of light and dark into a pattern of electric signals. The signals carry the code to a computer. No matter which direction the bar code goes across the slots, the computer can figure out the code.

A UPC cash register never makes a mistake, and it can do more than add up purchases accurately and quickly. The computer can also tell the brand name of each item, so the register can print the name of each item with the price on the register tape.

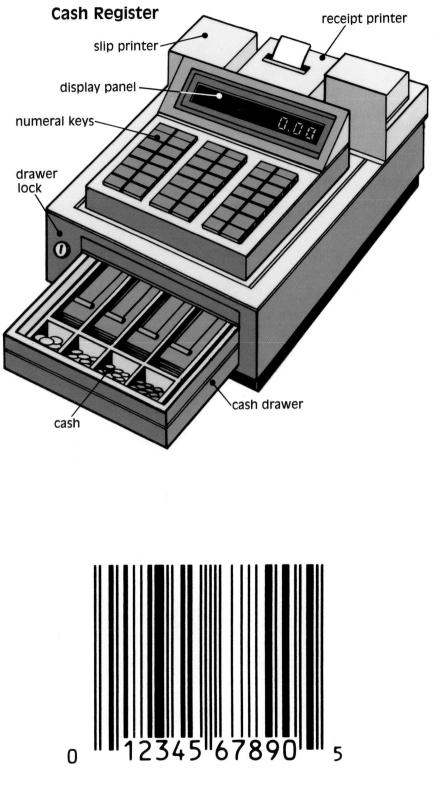

Cash Register

slip printer · receipt printer · display panel · numeral keys · drawer lock · cash · cash drawer

0 12345 67890 5

On the Go

If you could go anywhere in the world, where would you go? What type of transportation would you use?

You could use space-age transportation, such as supersonic planes and super-speedy trains, or you could use a good old bike.

Bicycle

The muscles and bones in your legs can produce a great deal of power, but not much speed. The fastest a human can run is about twenty miles an hour. A bicycle lets you travel faster and farther than you can ever run on foot, even though you use the same leg muscles for running and bike riding.

When you push your bike's pedals around once, the pedal *sprocket,* the wheel with teeth, also goes around once. At the same time, the small rear wheel sprocket, connected by a chain, goes around more than once, and turns the rear wheel the same number of times.

If you are traveling uphill on a bike, it becomes more difficult to pedal. You can get more strength at the back of the wheel by having it turn fewer times every time you turn the pedals. That's why there are bikes with gears that can change. Many bikes have several sprockets of different sizes at the pedals and at the rear wheel. Levers move the chain sideways so that it can slip from sprocket to sprocket. If you have two sprockets at the pedals and five at the wheel, that makes 10 different combinations of big and little sprockets—a 10-speed bike.

When you pedal very slowly, your bike wobbles or even falls. But when you move fast or travel uphill, it balances. When a wheel turns around an axle, all its weight is thrown outward in the direction the wheel is pointed. If you try to turn the wheel right or left, or if you try to make the wheel fall over sideways, it resists the change. To make the wheel change direction, you have to push against the weight going in the original direction. This force in two bicycle wheels is strong enough to keep you from falling over.

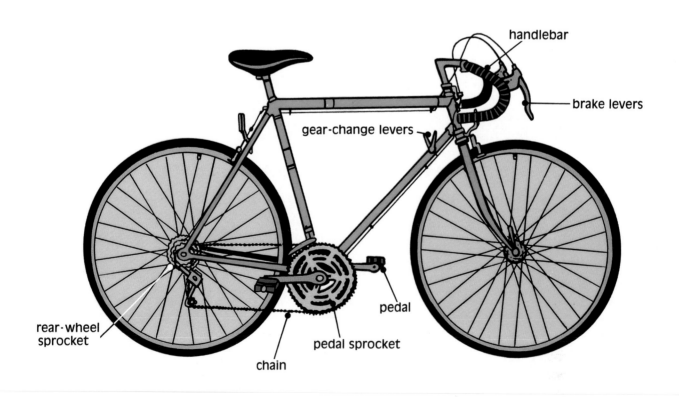

handlebar

brake levers

gear-change levers

pedal

rear-wheel sprocket

pedal sprocket

chain

Elevator

Elevators make tall buildings possible. Some elevators carry people and freight up by pushing. Others do it by pulling.

In some buildings a pushing elevator will work. The elevator box sits on top of a metal column that slides inside a tube. The column and tube go as far down into the ground as the elevator goes high. A pump turned by an electric motor pushes oil from a storage tank into the space at the bottom of the tube. The oil then pushes the metal column up. For the elevator to come back down again, a kind of faucet opens to let oil flow back into the storage tank. This is an especially safe kind of elevator, because the elevator box is always held up by the metal column.

In taller buildings, elevators are pulled up by cables. An electric motor does part of the pulling upward—but only part. The cable goes up from the elevator box and wraps around a pulley that is turned by the motor. Then the cable goes down again from the pulley and is attached to a large weight that slides up and down. This weight balances the weight of the box.

A cable-operated elevator has to have a safety system to take over if the cables break. Most often, a hook attached to the elevator box is used. This hook is automatically released when the elevator starts going down too fast. The hook catches on the side of the elevator shaft and holds the box steady until rescuers can get to it.

Stopping an elevator at the right floor is done with a simple electrical memory. When you push the button for the floor you want, an electrical message goes to a control box which can tell how many floors the elevator must go. As it moves, a switch trips to indicate that the elevator has come to another floor. If you are on the first floor and you want to go to the

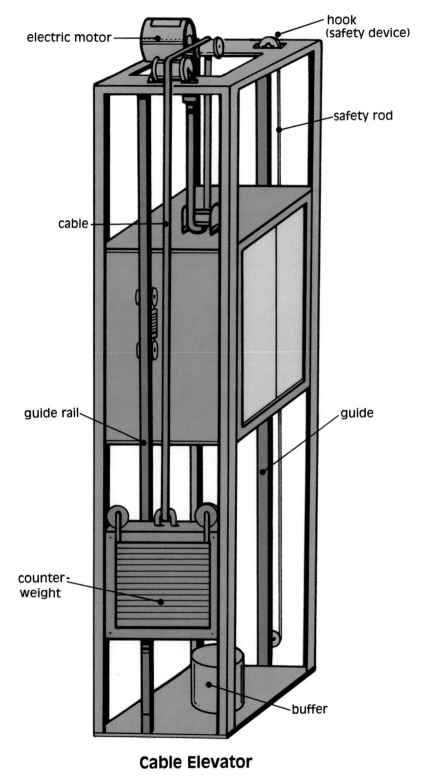

Cable Elevator

18th floor, you push the 18 button, and that tells the memory to wait for 17 messages before stopping the motor and opening the doors.

Automobile

All automobiles are much the same. They have:

- a motor for power,
- a way to get the motor's power to the wheels,
- a way to change the speed,
- a way to control direction,
- a way to stop.

Most automobiles use an *internal-combustion engine*. *Combustion* means burning. An internal-combustion engine is one that produces power by burning fuel inside it.

The fuel used in most automobiles is gasoline. Gasoline is a liquid that burns quickly. When a spark is set to gasoline, the gasoline burns so fast that it explodes. An internal combustion engine controls the power of exploding gasoline. When an automobile speeds along the highway, thousands of explosions every minute power the driving wheels.

To make gasoline explode, it has to be sprayed in a fine vapor and mixed with air. This happens in the *carburetor*. A spark plug makes an electric spark at just the right time to explode the gasoline vapor.

An automobile engine usually has four, six, or eight *cylinders*. Each cylinder is a smooth round hole in a block of metal. In each of these cylinders, a *piston* slides up and down. When gasoline explodes inside the cylinder, it drives the piston down. This is what turns the explosive heat of gasoline into the motion of a machine.

The power goes from the engine to the wheels through *shafts* and *gears*. A shaft is a rod that turns. A gear is a wheel with notches, called teeth or cogs, around its edge. Gears are attached to shafts inside a gearbox. The gearbox is called the *transmission*. It transmits, or sends, the power from the motor to the shaft that drives the wheels. The notches of the gears fit together, so that the movement of one gear turns another gear. Gears can be used to change the speed of the car and help the car to start or to climb hills.

Gears are needed in a car because an internal combustion engine works well only when it is running at high speed. But when a car is started, its wheels must go slowly and build to a higher speed. Gears are used to do this. At first, or low gear, small gears turn larger gears. The smaller gears must turn many times to make the larger gears turn once in the same period of time. So, the larger gear turns more slowly than the smaller one and makes the car's wheels turn slowly.

As a car picks up speed, its driver changes the gears so that the engine can make the wheels go faster. Gears also change the direction in which a shaft turns. When a driver wants to back up a car, the driver changes the gears and puts them into reverse. In cars with *automatic transmissions,* the gears change automatically. That means the engine's power always turns the wheels at the speed that is needed.

Another set of gears called the *differential* transmits power from the drive shaft to the *axles*. The axles are the shafts on which pairs of wheels revolve. The differential also allows the car to make smooth turns. When a car goes around a corner, the outside wheels have to go further than the inside wheels. The gears in the differential allow the outer wheel to go faster than the inner one.

How can a driver stop a car? The driver steps on the brake pedal. This makes a *brake shoe* rub against a smooth part inside each wheel. The car slows. The power of the driver's foot pushing down on the brake pedal travels to the brake through tubes filled with oil. The oil is squeezed by the brake pedal and it pushes equally on each of the brakes.

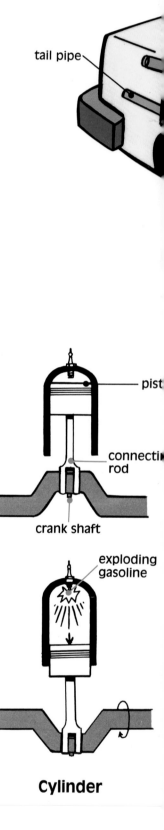

tail pipe

pist

connectin rod

crank shaft

exploding gasoline

Cylinder

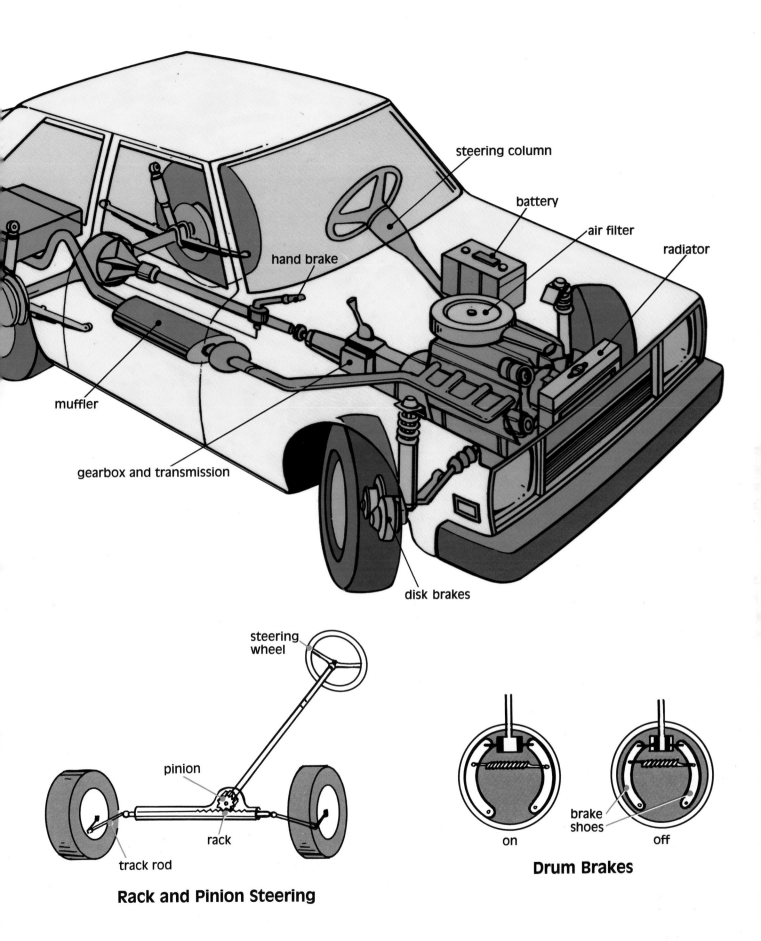

steering column

battery

air filter

radiator

hand brake

muffler

gearbox and transmission

disk brakes

steering wheel

pinion

rack

track rod

Rack and Pinion Steering

brake shoes

on

off

Drum Brakes

Train

A locomotive is a kind of giant tractor that runs on tracks and is used to pull trains. Two different kinds of motors can power modern locomotives—the electric motor and the diesel engine.

Electric locomotives are used in places where many trains run over the same tracks for short distances. Electric current flows through wires that are carried above the tracks. The train connects with the wire to get power for the locomotive's motors.

Diesel engines usually provide the power for locomotives that travel long distances. In most ways, a diesel engine is like a gasoline engine. Explosions inside the engine drive pistons in cylinders. The pistons move up and down to turn a crank and deliver power. But a diesel engine uses fuel oil instead of gasoline and it has no spark plugs to make the fuel explode.

Instead of making a fuel and air mixture in a carburetor, a diesel engine pumps the fuel directly into the cylinder and makes the mixture right there. The most important difference between a diesel and any other kind of engine is in the way it makes the fuel explode.

When a gas is squeezed into a small space, its particles hit each other with great speed. As they do this they make heat. The pistons in a diesel engine quickly squeeze the fuel and air mixture so tight that it becomes hot enough to explode.

When a diesel engine is used to power a locomotive, it does not drive the wheels directly. The motor turns a generator to produce electricity, which is stored in huge rechargeable batteries. The electricity drives electric motors that are connected directly to each wheel of the locomotive.

The reason for using electric motors is that, unlike internal combustion engines,

Diesel Train

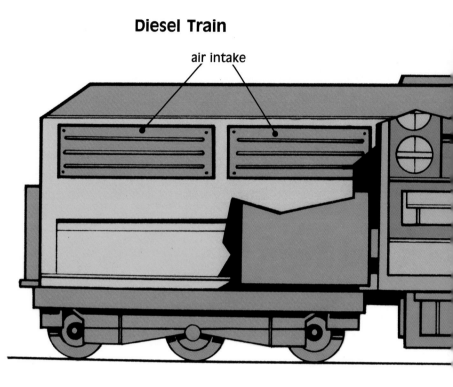

air intake

Electric Train

electric motors can produce great power at very low speeds. Because a diesel locomotive uses electric motors to deliver the power to the wheels, it does not have to have a transmission and shift gears as it picks up speed.

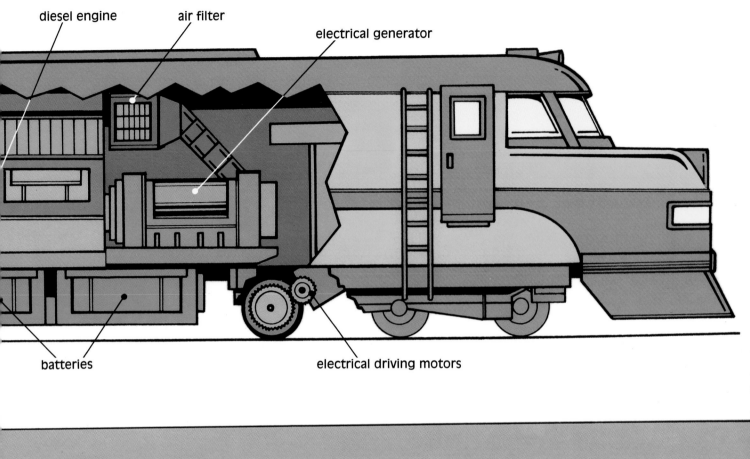

diesel engine   air filter

electrical generator

batteries

electrical driving motors

The Japanese bullet train, the world's fastest, reaches speeds of more than 100 miles an hour (160 kph). Many ordinary railroad trains go about half that speed.

Boat

Boats need power to push their way through water. Muscle power can move small boats, but not very far or very fast. Wind power can move small boats swiftly and large boats a long distance, but only when there is enough wind in the right direction. A strong motor is needed to make large boats move fast and carry great cargoes directly to their destinations.

Smaller boats usually have gasoline engines. Bigger ones often have diesel motors, like those that drive locomotives. And the great ships that cross the oceans have power plants that use the modern kind of steam engine called a *turbine*. They get heat from oil or coal or even from nuclear power.

Motors move boats and ships by turning their propellers. A propeller acts like a winged screw boring though the water in a spiral. As the propeller's slanted blades turn in a spiral, they push the water backward and the boat moves forward.

Ships and most boats do not go very fast. That is because the power that drives them forward must push aside the weight of the water through which the hull is moving. The water pushes back and drags along the sides. Boats that go fast are designed to ride as high in the water as possible.

A speedboat with a powerful engine has a hull shaped to rise out of the water as it goes faster. At top speed, it looks as if it is sliding on top of the water, with only its propeller below the surface.

Hydrofoil   Two other kinds of boats are able to ride above the water. One of these boats is called a hydrofoil. It has winglike fins below the hull that slice through the water. At high speed these fins lift the main part of the boat completely out of the water.

Hovercraft   The second boat that can ride free of the water is called a hovercraft. A hovercraft is powered by huge fans pointed downward. As they blow toward the water, they raise the boat on a cushion of air, and it hovers above the surface. Propellers on top push the hovercraft forward.

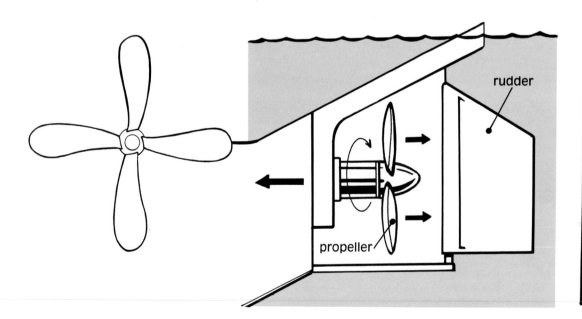

Speedboat

rudder

propeller

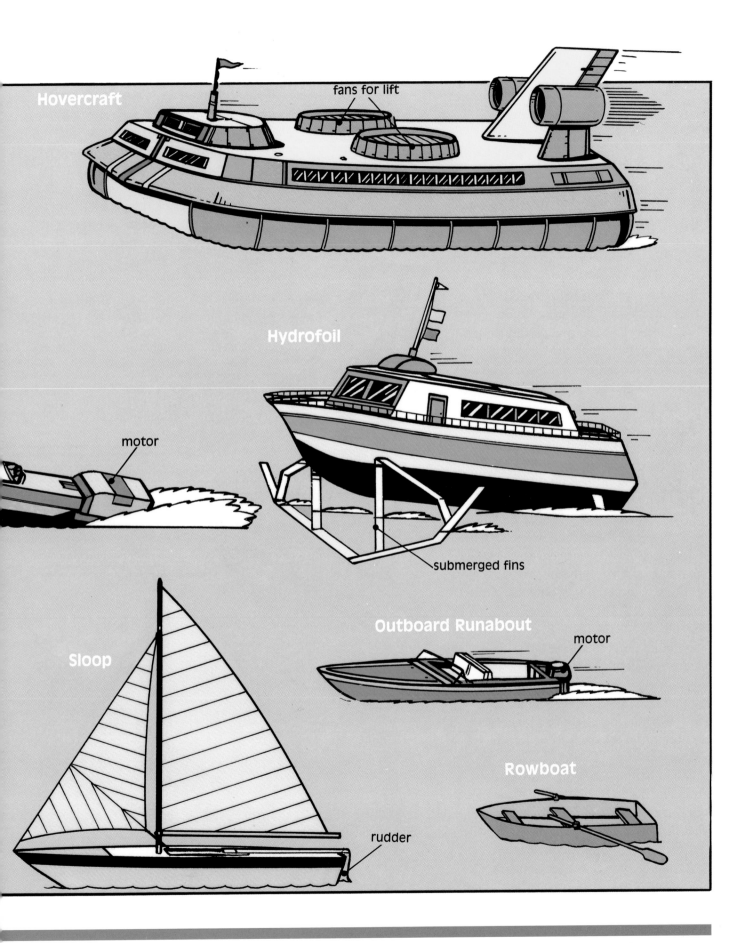

Hovercraft

fans for lift

Hydrofoil

motor

submerged fins

Sloop

Outboard Runabout

motor

Rowboat

rudder

Airplane

Human beings have always dreamed of flying. At first they tried to invent flying machines that imitated birds with wings that flap. These early machines didn't work. A much simpler kind of wing turned out to work very well. This wing didn't flap at all, but it gave plenty of lift when it was moved through the air by a gasoline engine and a propeller.

The shape of the wing makes it able to lift an airplane off the ground. The wing is flat on the bottom, but curved on top. When it slices through the air, the air has to go farther to get around the curved top surface. The air has to "stretch out" to get over the wing, so there are fewer particles of air. The air above the wing weighs less and has less pressure than the air below the wing. The greater pressure of the air under the wing pushes up and keeps the plane from falling.

An airplane also uses the force of moving air to keep it flying straight and to make it change direction. Most planes have a three-part tail. The upright part is called the *fin* and the two side parts are called the *stabilizers*. They drag backward and keep the nose of the plane pointing ahead. The rear edges of the three tail parts have panels that swing on hinges. These steer the plane. When these panels are set at an angle, the wind pushes harder against them. If the tail is pushed in one direction, the nose of the plane is turned in the opposite direction.

Two different kinds of engines power airplanes, piston engines, and jet engines. A piston engine is used to turn a propeller, which works in the air much the same way a boat propeller works in water.

Most large planes use jet engines. A jet engine forces the plane forward by blasting

a continuous explosion of burning fuel out the rear.

The jet engine is a tube with air going in the front end. Fuel is sprayed into the air as it passes through, and the fuel is made to burn by a kind of spark plug. As the exploding fuel roars out the back, the plane is pushed forward.

There are different kinds of jet engines. The most usual one is called a *turbojet*. A turbojet uses some of its power to turn a fan, which sucks additional air into the front opening of the engine. More air means more fuel can burn, and this gives the jet even greater power.

rudder

tailfin

rear engine exhaust

stabilizer

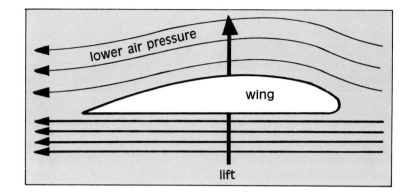

lower air pressure

wing

lift

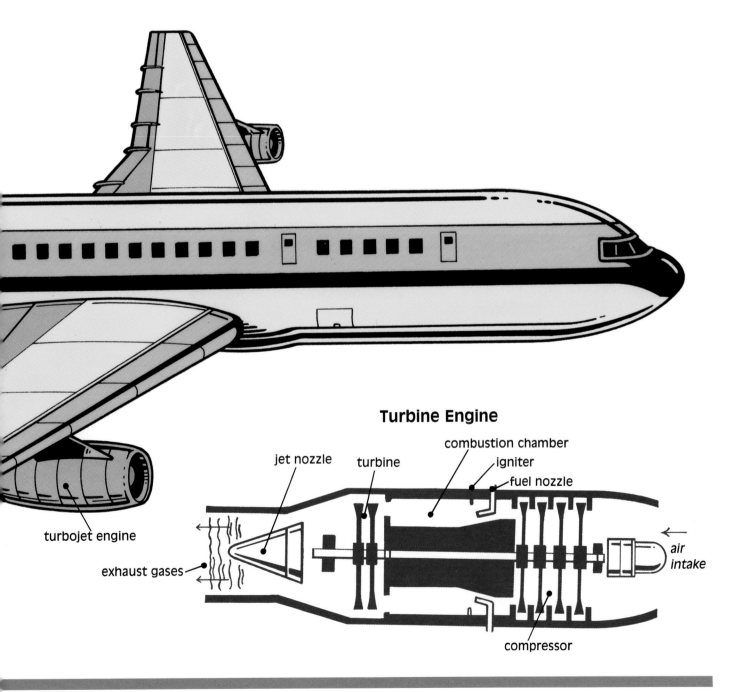

turbojet engine

Turbine Engine

jet nozzle

turbine

combustion chamber

igniter

fuel nozzle

air intake

exhaust gases

compressor

Helicopter A helicopter is a flying machine with moving wings. These wings, which are located above the body of the aircraft, are called *rotors*. The rotors lift the helicopter off the ground by whirling like a propeller pointed upward. The rotor turns on a shaft that comes up from the engine through the top of the helicopter.

The pilot can make the rotor spin faster or slower to make the machine go up or down. The pilot can also change the tilt of the rotor blades. This changes the amount of lift, even though the speed of the blades' spin remains the same.

What's more, the pilot can change the tilt of each rotor blade separately and very quickly. This is what makes the helicopter move forward or backward. To move forward, the pilot adds more lift to each blade when it is at the rear. To fly backward, the pilot adds lift to the rotor blades in front.

To change the direction in which the helicopter is moving, the pilot controls a second set of blades that rotate at the tail of the helicopter. If the helicopter didn't have this tail rotor, its body would move in the opposite direction when the big lifting rotor turns. The tail rotor balances the craft by pushing the air against the twisting force of the main rotors. Most of the time the tail rotor spins at just the right speed and angle to keep the helicopter pointing ahead. To make a turn, the pilot changes the tilt of the tail blades a little. They push either more or less against the twist of the helicopter to point the nose in a new direction.

tail rotor

stabilizer fin

tail rotor drive shaft

How a Helicopter Changes Direction

By changing the pitch of its rotor blades, a helicopter can change direction.

straight up or hovering

forward flight

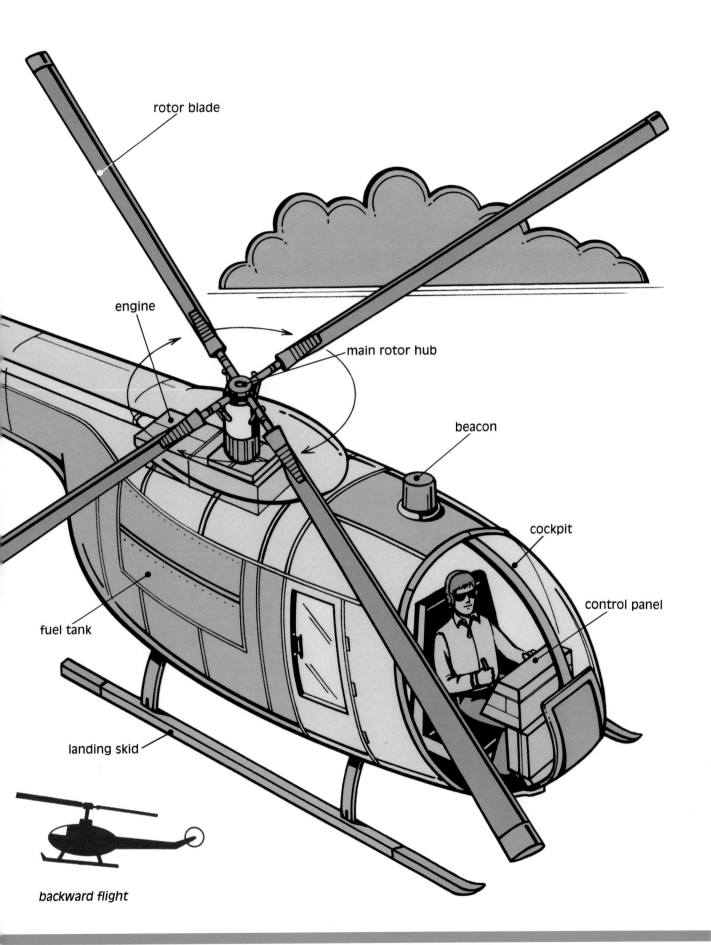

rotor blade

engine

main rotor hub

beacon

cockpit

control panel

fuel tank

landing skid

backward flight

Musical Instruments

How many different kinds of musical instruments can you find in this picture?

Some instruments are much the same today as they were 100 years ago. Others are newly invented.

Percussion

Percussion instruments make sound by striking, shaking, or scraping. Drums are played with the bang of a stick on a skin, called a *head,* stretched to cover openings on a cylinder or kettle. The sound vibrations caused by the sticks are *resonated,* or echoed, and made louder by the cylinder or kettle. Some small drums, called snare drums, have wires or catgut strings stretched tightly across the head at the cylinder bottom. These add a buzzing sound to the vibrations.

Bells Bells are a kind of percussion instrument that can make a tune. When a bell is hit, it makes a clear, single musical sound. The size and weight of the metal make the bell vibrate a certain number of times each second. By using different-sized bells, tunes can be played. One instrument that makes bell sounds is the *glockenspiel,* a German word that means *bell play.* Metal bars of different lengths and weights are struck by a hammer, vibrating in a bell-like way.

Other percussion instruments with bell-like sounds are the xylophone and marimba. The xylophone has wooden bars, which are struck by mallets. Each wooden bar sounds a different musical note. The sound vibrations of the bars are resonated by metal tubes. The marimba is a xylophone with many more wooden bars so that more complicated music can be played. It also has larger resonating tubes.

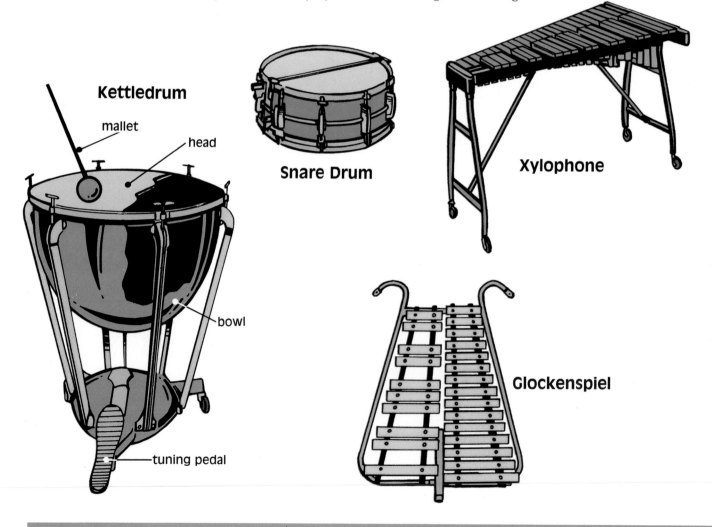

Kettledrum

mallet

head

bowl

tuning pedal

Snare Drum

Xylophone

Glockenspiel

Piano When you press piano keys, you operate levers that make small padded hammers hit tightly stretched wire strings. The wires vibrate when the hammers hit them. These vibrating wires are strung across a frame that is attached to a sounding board. When the strings vibrate, the sounding board vibrates, too, and this makes the sound louder. Different notes are heard because the strings vary in length and thickness. The shorter and thinner the wire, the higher the note.

Pianos are made in such a way that the length of time that wires vibrate can be controlled. That way, a musical note can be short and crisp or made to sound out for a longer time.

When you press a key, a damper pad lifts off the wires while levers make a hammer jump up and strike a wire. When you lift your finger off the key, the damper again presses against the wires to stop vibrations. So, to make a note short, the pianist lifts his or her fingers quickly.

Foot pedals also help the piano player control the vibrations by lifting the dampers or changing the way the hammers hit the wires.

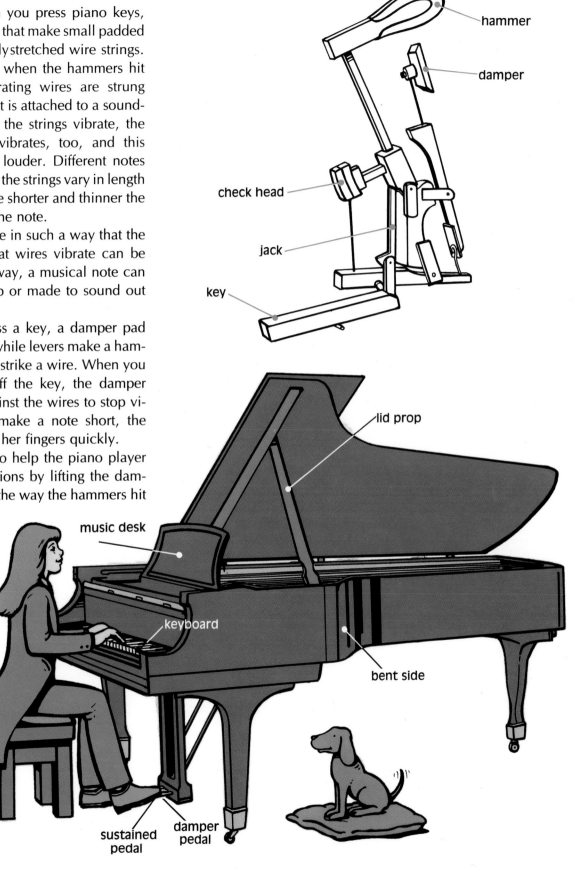

Whistle

Flute   To play a flute, you make your lips form an air passage so that you can blow across the edge of the *mouthpiece.* When you blow past this edge at just the right angle, the straight flow of the air is broken, and the air vibrates. The vibration in the air is a musical note. (The same thing happens when you pucker your lips to whistle.)

The low or high *pitch* of the sound that comes from the flute is partly determined by the size of the instrument. The shorter the instrument, the higher the note. A little piccolo plays higher notes than a full-size flute. But even more important, the length of the instrument's *sounding tube* can be changed, so you can change the pitch and play tunes. On a flute, you press levers that open and close holes in the tube. This makes the closed part of the tube shorter or longer.

Recorder   The recorder is another kind of whistle instrument that plays different notes when you open and close holes along the length of its sounding tube. To play a recorder you do not have to shape your lips to blow through the mouthpiece. The right shape of the air passage is built into the mouthpiece.

Organ   Pipe organs are whistle instruments, with one tube for each note. A keyboard, which looks much like a piano keyboard, works valves that let air blow through the openings of the tubes for the notes you play. The air comes from a compressor driven by an electric motor.

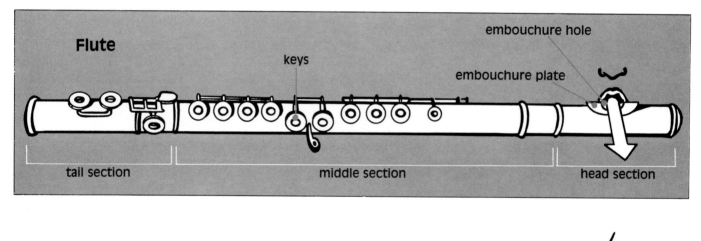

Flute — tail section, middle section, keys, embouchure hole, embouchure plate, head section

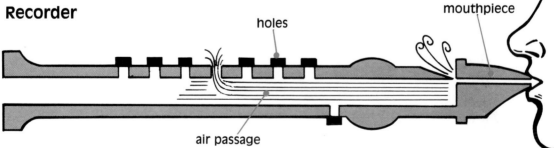

Recorder — holes, air passage, mouthpiece

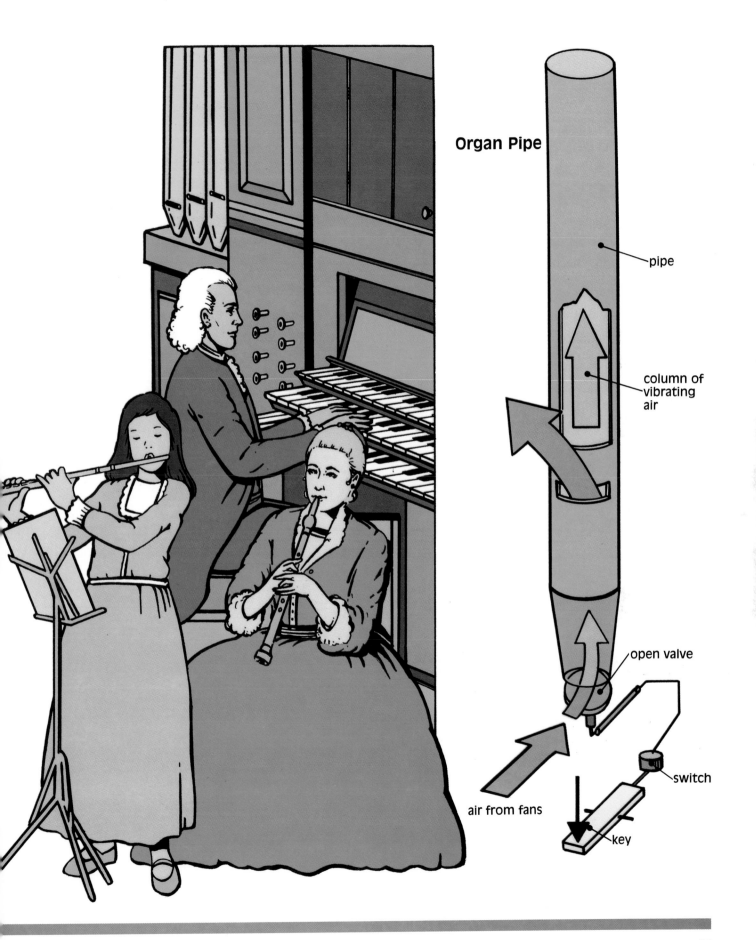

Organ Pipe

pipe

column of vibrating air

open valve

air from fans

switch

key

Brass

Bugles, trumpets, cornets, and various kinds of horns are called brass instruments. They are made of metal. They have a small cup-shaped mouthpiece at one end and a bell-like opening at the other.

Bugle The bugle is the simplest type of brass instrument. It is one long piece of curved tube with mouthpiece and bell. Like all brass instruments, it makes musical notes with the vibrations of the musician's lips. When the musician blows through tightened lips into the mouthpiece, the vibrations go through the tube and become resonated. Bugle players change the notes from low to high by changing the tightness of their lips as they blow into the mouthpiece. Because the notes depend on the shape of the bugle player's lips, the number of notes he or she can play is limited. Other brass instruments can play many more notes because they have ways of controlling the flow of sound vibrations.

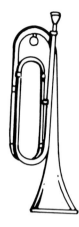

Bugle

Valve Instruments Brass valve instruments work just like the bugle, with one big difference. With a valve instrument, the musician's lips get help in making notes of different pitch. The help comes from valves which are pressed down to shorten and lengthen the amount of tubing through which the lip vibrations pass. When the length of the tubes is changed, the notes change. And so a player of a trumpet or other valve instrument can play almost any note.

Slide Trombone One brass instrument, the slide trombone, has a different way of changing the length of the sound tube, however. Instead of valves, it has a long sliding part. One piece of tube slips over another, and the musician changes notes by moving the slide out and in.

mouthpiece

valve

fingerhold

bell

water key

tuning slide

Trumpet

Reed

Reed instruments are also called *wood-winds* because some were once made of wood. Clarinets, saxophones, and oboes are well-known modern-day reed instruments. These instruments make music through vibrations of pieces of wood cut into a long thin wedge. This wedge is called a *reed*. When you hold the reed tightly between your lips and blow against its sharp, flexible edge, the reed vibrates and sounds a note.

Clarinet   A clarinet is a straight tube, with many holes and keys to shut and open with your fingers to change the notes.

Saxophone   Saxophones come in the shape of the letter *j*. They come in different sizes. They work the same way as a clarinet, with a single reed and many keys to press. Two other instruments use a pair of reeds instead of just one. They are the oboe and the bassoon. The two reeds vibrate against each other between the musician's lips.

Harmonica   A harmonica is a reed instrument that has many separate metal reeds, one for each note. The reeds vibrate only when air goes one way past them, so each hole in a harmonica has two reeds pointed in opposite directions. This way each hole can produce two notes—one when the player blows air out, and another when the player sucks air in.

Accordions and concertinas also have reeds that are similar to those of a harmonica. But the air is supplied by bellows. They are pushed by the player's arms.

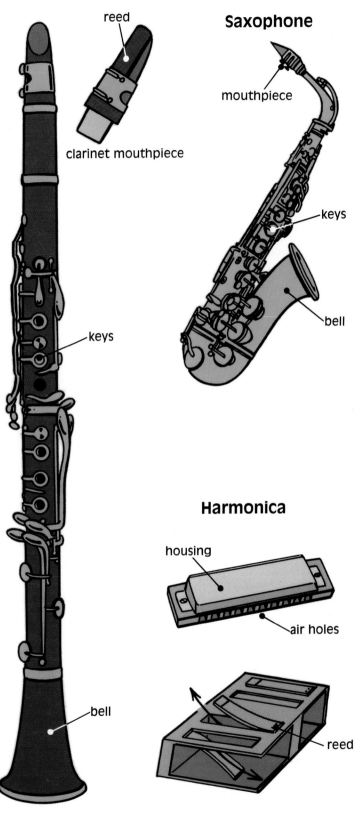

Clarinet

reed

clarinet mouthpiece

keys

bell

Saxophone

mouthpiece

keys

bell

Harmonica

housing

air holes

reed

String

String instruments make music with vibrations of strings, which can be bowed (rubbed with a bow) or plucked. The body of the instrument is hollow and acts like an amplifier.

Bowed/Plucked Instruments

The violin is an example of a bowed instrument. The musician uses a bow with tight, coarse hairs to rub across the strings of a violin. The hairs of the bow are coated with *rosin,* a sticky sap from a tree. As the musician draws the bow across the violin strings, the rosin sticks for an instant and pulls the string. Then the rosin lets go and the string jumps back, making the vibration of a musical note.

To change the note of a violin string, a musician changes its length by pressing the string tightly with a finger against the neck of the instrument. Only the part of the string below the finger is left free to vibrate. The shorter the vibrating part of the string is, the higher the note.

Other instruments, such as the viola, work the same way.

Plucked instruments—such as guitars, banjos, and harps—are played without a bow. The musician plucks the strings with fingertips or strums the strings with fingernails or a pick.

Electric Guitar
Some string instruments have an electric amplifier. The amplifier is similar to the one that makes a radio or phonograph work. The strings vibrate close to an electrical *pickup.* The vibrating metal of the strings changes the current flowing through the pickup. The pickup sends the changing electrical signals to the amplifier to make the sounds of the guitar much louder.

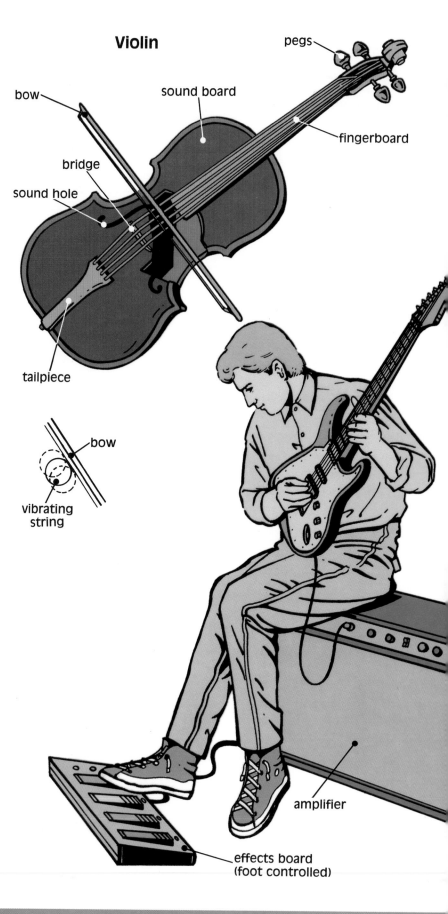

Violin

pegs

bow

sound board

fingerboard

bridge

sound hole

tailpiece

bow

vibrating string

amplifier

effects board
(foot controlled)

Electronic

Modern electronic equipment can now copy very accurately the sounds made by musical instruments. Machines that do this are called *synthesizers*. They make up, or synthesize, musical sounds by creating electrical signals that duplicate the vibrations made by musical instruments. When these signals are amplified and played through a loudspeaker, they sound like real musical instruments.

A synthesizer is played with a keyboard like a piano, but it can be made to sound like a brass or whistle or string instrument—or a drum—because the electronic circuits can reproduce the special variations that each kind of instrument gives to the notes.

A synthesizer can also create musical effects that no musical instrument can do alone. And it can combine the sounds of many instruments. A synthesizer has a computer memory. You can play a piece of music so that it sounds like a violin, then play that piece back from the computer's memory. While the tune is playing back, you can play it again with the sound of a flute or a trumpet, and you can put that in the computer's memory, too. A synthesizer can sound like an entire orchestra playing at once.

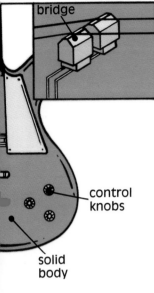

bridge

control knobs

solid body

Electric Guitar

Synthesizer

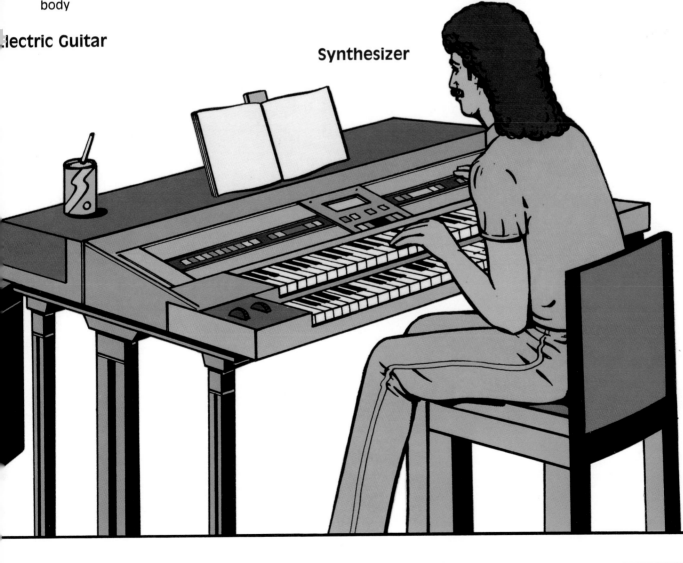

Medical Machines

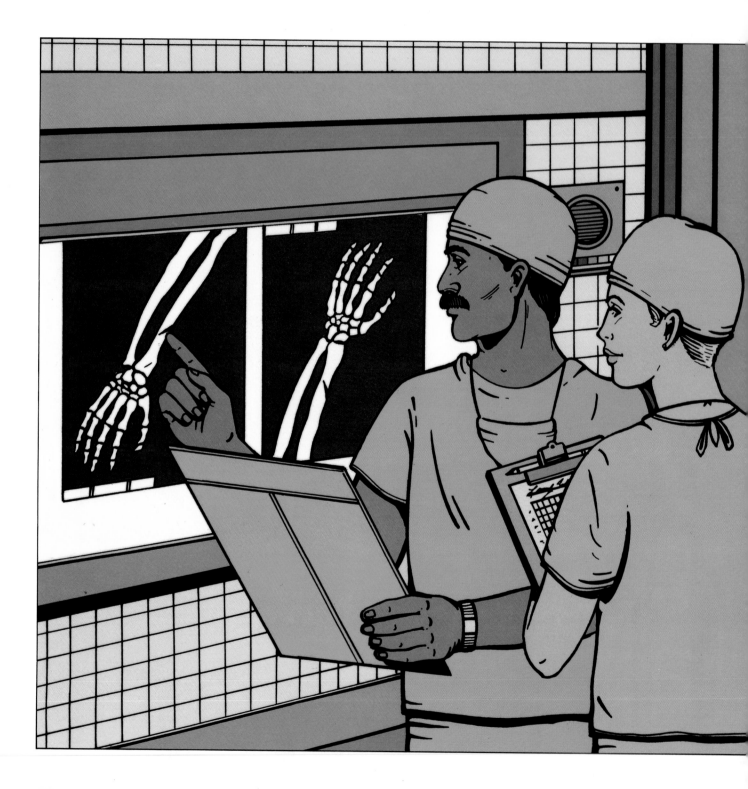

Some medical machines make surgery unnecessary. Others help make it easier and less painful.

Recent medical developments offer people with physical problems a chance to lead normal and active lives.

X ray

The X-ray machine makes it possible for doctors to look into the human body and see bones, muscles, and organs. This machine is a kind of camera that records a picture on film coated with chemicals. But this camera does not use ordinary light to take pictures. It uses *X rays,* a form of light energy that cannot be seen by the eye.

X rays come from a high-energy electrical tube. This tube uses a strong electrical current. Inside the tube, a beam of electric particles is aimed at a metal target. When the particles smash into the target, they create X rays powerful enough to pass through solid objects, such as a body.

Like visible light, X rays pass through some things more easily than through others. When these rays are aimed at a hard and dense object, such as a bone, not all the rays get through. So the bone shows up as a dark shadow on the X-ray film when it is developed. Body organs—heart, lungs, and stomach—show up as lighter shadows. A doctor may study these shadows on film to learn what is happening to a patient's body.

X rays are dangerous. Their high energy, if it is absorbed, can damage parts of the body they pass through, so doctors use X rays as little as possible. Another problem: An X-ray photograph combines the shadows of separate parts of the body on the flat surface of the film. A doctor may not be able to tell exactly where the trouble is inside the body.

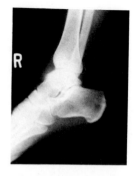

This is an X ray of a woman's ankle.

X-Ray Machine

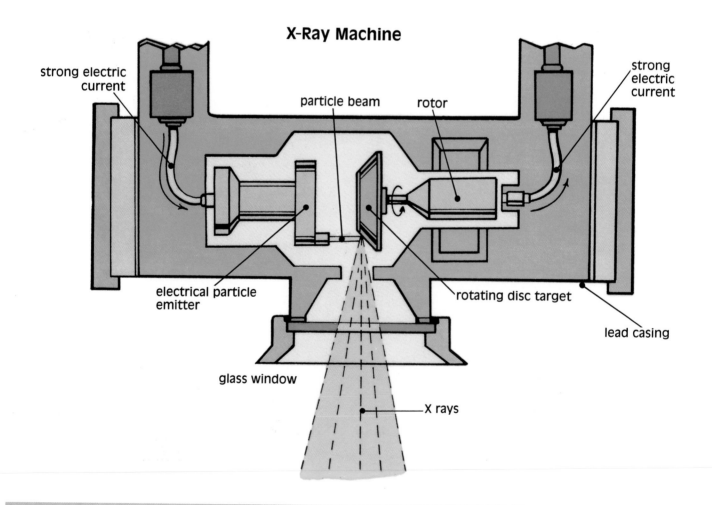

strong electric current

particle beam

rotor

strong electric current

electrical particle emitter

rotating disc target

lead casing

glass window

X rays

Tomography To avoid these problems, doctors may use a more complicated kind of X-ray machine. It is called a *tomograph* machine. *Tomo* means slice. This kind of X ray can take a picture of a thin section of the inside of a body, so that a doctor can pinpoint exactly what the physical problem is—and where it is. The tomograph machine beams rays from different directions at the same place inside the body. The energy is concentrated on the flat section where the rays cross each other, and this is the slice that shows up clearly on the X-ray film.

Tomography can also be less dangerous than regular X-ray photography. Since the X rays come from different directions, fewer rays go through most parts of the body. Only the section being examined gets the full strength of X rays.

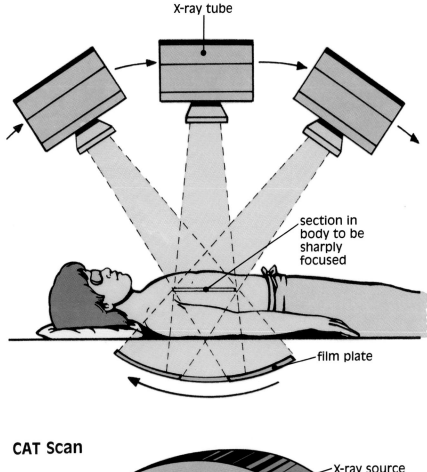

X-ray tube

section in body to be sharply focused

film plate

CAT Scan *CAT* stands for computerized *axial* tomography, a way to get a super-sharp picture of a section of the human body. It uses a computer. This machine uses many narrow beams instead of a wide X-ray beam to take a photo on film. The narrow beams—as many as 160—are shot through the body from different angles. These beams hit an electric sensor, which records the X-ray energy as an electrical message. The message goes to a computer. Each separate X-ray beam records some information. The computer takes all the bits of information and pieces them together. The result is a picture, which is displayed on a television screen.

Using a CAT scan, doctors can take separate pictures of many sections of the body right next to each other. These sections—like thin slices of an onion laid side by side—can be looked at in sequence to get a full three-dimensional picture of what is going on inside the body.

CAT Scan

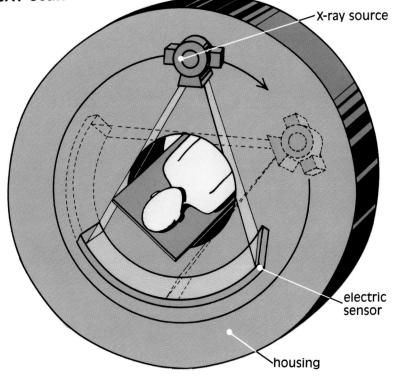

X-ray source

electric sensor

housing

Fiber Optics Doctors can also see inside the body with a thin tube filled with flexible glass fibers. The tube can be inserted into an opening in the body or into a blood vessel. Then the tube can be gently pushed until it reaches the place that must be examined.

Laser light can travel around corners inside the long thin glass fibers. A doctor can clearly see what the end of the tube is pointed at. The doctor can then push tiny tools through the tube to perform an operation.

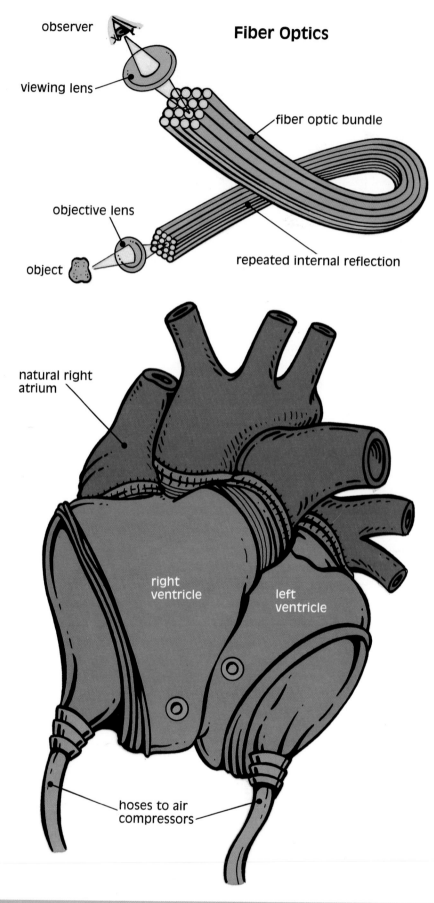

Fiber Optics

observer

viewing lens

fiber optic bundle

objective lens

object

repeated internal reflection

natural right atrium

right ventricle

left ventricle

hoses to air compressors

Artificial Heart

When a heart is damaged, surgery can often repair it. But, sometimes, a living heart cannot be fixed. That is when doctors try to find a replacement for it. They may replace the original heart with the heart of a healthy person who has just died in an accident.

A human heart is hard to find. That is why doctors are now experimenting with mechanical hearts.

A mechanical, or artificial, heart is a pump. Like a real heart, it pushes blood through blood vessels. The blood carries nourishment and oxygen to every part of the body.

A living heart uses muscles for power. An artificial heart, made mostly of plastic, uses the power of compressed air. (Compressed air is also used to pump bicycle and car tires.)

Tubes from an air compressor are attached through the patient's chest. The patient can move around only with this machine attached. Because of this, an artificial heart is clumsy. So it is usually used only to keep a patient alive while doctors seek a living heart.

Kidney Dialysis

The human kidney is another organ that sometimes fails completely. A person whose kidneys have failed completely may die unless a replacement kidney can be found.

The replacement kidney must come from another human. All healthy people have two kidneys. So some people, often relatives of an ill person, are willing to give one of their kidneys as a lifesaver.

But some people with kidney disease are kept alive with an artificial kidney. It is called a *dialysis* machine. A dialysis machine is too large to be put inside a human body. The machine is attached to the patient by tubes.

Kidneys clean waste products from the blood. Every drop of blood in a person's body flows through the kidneys. After the waste is separated from the blood, it flows out of the body in urine.

People without kidneys must have their blood cleaned several times a week. Their blood flows through a tube that leads from the body and through the dialysis machine. A complicated set of filters in the machine remove the poisonous chemicals and other wastes. Then clean blood flows back into the body.

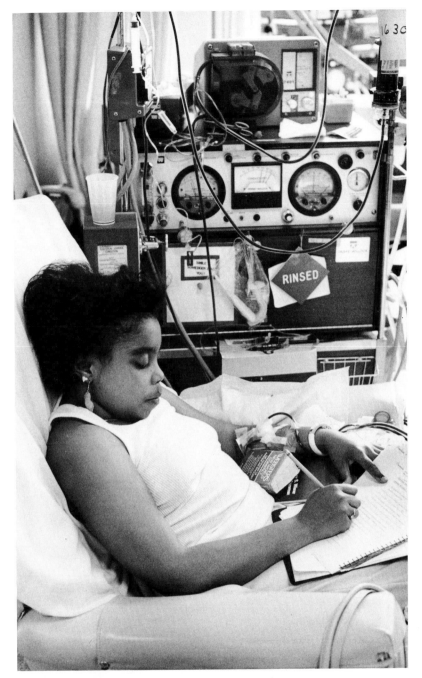

A Pennsylvania student does schoolwork as she undergoes kidney dialysis treatment.

Artificial Limb

Machines can replace real arms and legs that must be removed. One such machine is called the *Boston arm*. It was invented in a hospital in Boston, Massachusetts.

A mechanical arm is made of many small parts that all work together. Midget electric motors powered by batteries turn gears. These gears can make a mechanical elbow bend, a mechanical wrist twist, and mechanical fingers grasp and open.

In a living arm, nerves connected to the brain send tiny electrical messages that make muscles work. The muscles tighten and relax and move each section of the arm and hand.

With an electric artificial arm, the brain and nerves and muscles also play a part. Each of the electric motors in the artificial arm is turned on and off by the same kind of messages that guide the movement of a living arm. The brain sends electrical messages to the muscles in the part of the living arm that remains. Wires attached to these muscles pick up the tiny electric signals and send them to the arm. Inside the arm these signals are made strong enough to turn switches on and off. These switches make the mechanical arm's motors turn on and off when the brain tells them to.

With practice, a person who has lost a living arm can learn to work several motors in different directions at once. An artificial arm can do many of the useful jobs that a living arm can.

Boston Arm

Index to Diagrams and Illustrations

Index